How To Swing Trade

A Step-by-Step Guide on How to Make a Living from Passive Income and Become a Successful Swing Trader

Warren Johnson

Table of Contents

Introduction

This book is dedicated to any individual who has an interest in swing trading and they need to be successful in that field.

You will learn about the definition of swing trading, the advantages, disadvantages, and how it works.

If you are a newbie in this kind of trade, do not panic all about starting swing trading is clearly explained. The amount of capital needed, the income that you can make from swing trading, your daily routine as a swing trader, and how you can start swing trading. You will also get all the tips need to start and be successful. There are different tools and techniques that are illustrated and will greatly help when it comes to swing trading. There are also different strategies and rules that need to be followed in order to succeed in swing trading. Money management is another very important concept that needs to be understood to help in the swing-trading journey. You will learn about the different mistakes, how to be a successful swing trader and the terms that are used.

Thank you for taking the time and picking this book as your final choice. All the efforts were put in to ensure you get a detailed and useful book. Enjoy your reading.

Chapter 1: What Is Swing Trading?

What is Swing Trading?

What's the first thing that comes in your mind when you hear about Swing trading? This is a type of fundamental trading where trade is held for more than a day. Some swing traders are fundamentalists, with corporate fundamentals change, which requires some days or week to bring enough price movement to make a decent profit. One week is a general time frame, and some trades take longer than a few months; however, this can still be considered as swing trades.

The aim of swing trading is to get a vast potential price move. Some traders prefer volatile stocks, while others prefer sedate stocks. Swing trading is a process of recognizing how an asset's price will move, entering a position, and getting a huge profit from that move. The goal of swing traders is to capture a lump of the expected price move and move on to the next opportunity.

Swing traders search for intermediate-term using various technical analysis. For you want to be successful in swing trading, you should familiarize yourself with technical analysis. Swing traders estimate trades on a risk- reward basis. Traders analyses the chart of an asset, determining where they will enter, where to place a stop loss, and predict the time to get out with a profit. For example, risking $1 per share on a setup to get a $3 gain, that will be a favorable risk/reward. They are also risking $1 to make $1 or $0.75 that isn't as favorable risk/reward. Due to the short-term of the trades, swing traders essentially use technical analysis.

Fundamental analysis enhances the analysis. Swing traders look for opportunities on daily charts and find exact entry and stop-loss points.

The Pros and Cons of Swing Trading

One way to trade financial markets is Swing trading. However, there are both advantages and disadvantages in any type of trading, and knowing all these ahead of time will be essential. To be able to make a wise decision before beginning.
In this chapter, I will point out some of the advantages and disadvantages of swing trading:

Advantages

- **More Time**

One main advantage of swing trading is that it saves time. For example, when intraday trading, a trader can check off all the positions immediately before the set-out time for trading while for swing trading, a trader has more time to square off the positions conveniently and not according to time. This type of trading does not need to be monitored constantly, so it is the best for investors who don't have a lot of time, for example, traders who have a full- time job and trade on a part-time basis. Once you have become proficient at technical analysis, and in line with the narrow focus at about a stock, identifying a key trade won't take too much time, and you will begin to make your trades.

- **No Sophisticated Tools**

Swing trading does not require sophisticated tools or algorithms, which is the case with intraday trading. Intraday trading is price and quickness of trading, and a trader will need tools to act swiftly in accordance with the price and volume action in a stock. Swing trading can be done without any sophisticated tools and can also be done by anyone. This trading does not require speed; however, it needs the correct analysis of the stock movement on the market.

- **Narrow Focus**

Swing trading is a technical and based on looking for short term trends where stocks quickly increase in value. The trade time frame lets you focus on the core market movement and identifies the trend momentum quickly. Also, you don't need to have information like the company's balance sheet or any other things in order to get the required information before you make a trade. This narrow focus will help you concentrate on a few keys areas to be good at.

Swing trading is all about the price and

trends. This also makes swing trading less stressful than other short-term trading such as Day Trading.

Disadvantages

- **Higher Margin Requirement**

Swing trading is about judgment, and when you are keeping positions open for some days than the margin requirement, it will be high since stock prices do not move according to your will. That's why this trading can only be done by people who have lots of cash. One of the factors that discourage people from becoming a swing trader is the higher margin requirement.

- **Risk of Loss**

Another disadvantage of swing trading is the risk of the stock moving in the opposite direction of the predicted move of the swing trader, and this will result in a loss for the trader. In other words, this type of trading does not offer guaranteed profits. In fact, the magnitude of the loss might be more significant than intraday trading.

- **No Rotation of Capital**

A swing trader is not able to rotate the capital, so they are only able to lock their capital into a single trade, which might give returns to the trader, or it might not. As opposed to trading such as intraday, which you can buy or sell stock as many times as you want, and you can rotate capital to get good returns.

As you can see from the advantages and disadvantages of swing trading, for a new trader thinking of doing this type of trading. You can now have a view of both sides of swing trading for you to make an informed decision.

How Does Swing Trading Work?

This is a trading that captures a swing or one move. The idea is to undergo as "little pain" as possible by leaving your trades before opposing pressure moves closer. This means booking your profits before the market reverses, and you lose your gains. Swing trading capitalizes on the upward and downward in the price of a security. You are hoping to capture small moves within a more significant trend and aiming to make a profit in five months while swing traders earn 5% gains a week and surpass other traders in the long run. The majority of swing traders use daily charts such as 60 minutes, 48 hours, 24 hours, etc. to pick the best entry or exit point. But some traders use a shorter time frame chart like a 4-hour or hourly chart.

Larger investment firms do not engage in swing trading, but individual traders take a swing trading approach to day-to-day market strategies. More large-sized trading firms have stock market positions too large to get in and out market trade on a time-sensitive basis.

Day Trading, Swing Trading, and Options Trading

Trading is one of the essential tasks, and it requires continuous efforts to understand and set up a trading system. The time frame to opt to trade will have a massive influence on the trading strategy and profitability. In day trading, you open and close multiple positions within a day while in swing trading, trades last for many days, weeks, or even months. These trading styles depend on the amount of capital available, time, psychology, and the trading market. All the trading styles are good, and it depends on which style suits a trader's personal circumstances.

- **Day Trading**

This is a type of trading where you buy and sell a security in a single trading day. For example, buying stock in the morning and selling the stock in the afternoon. Day trading can be done in any marketplace. Day trading can also be called intraday trading. Day trading is a highly skilled job and well- funded. Traders can hold amount for short term trading and increase any small change in price. You make multiple trades on a daily basis. Day traders don't hold positions overnight, and they opt to close their positions each evening and reopen them the following day. This is a short-term strategy that plans to profit from small intraday fluctuations in price, instead of a

long-term strategy. This trading is different from the traditional investing technique of purchasing low, waiting, and a higher sell. Day traders think differently from investors, and they focus on the asset price action than its long-term potential. The strategies of day trading are based on huge amounts of technical analysis, and they require the trader to be up to date with news that might cause market fluctuations.

- **Swing Trading**

Swing trading is a trading strategy where trade is held for several days in order to gain profit from price changes. The trading position is held more than a day trading position. You can seek your profits by either buying an asset or short selling. The trading uses technical analysis to determine the movement of a particular stock, either up or down at a specific time. By monitoring technical indicators, day traders look for stocks with momentum price movement signaling the best time to buy and sell.

This trading does not focus on the long-term market value of a stock. It is not possible to consistently pinpoint the correct high or low of every swing; however, you can capture the price movement. It's common to miss the accurate estimated highs or lows as it will take time to confirm if a new swing is underway.

- **Option Trading**

Investment is about buying stocks on the stock market. There are different terms in the stock market, such as options trading. One common strategy is to buy stocks and hold on them with the aim of making a long-term gain. This is the best way of investing as you get an idea of which stock you should buy, or you can seek the services of a broker who can advise and guide you on the matter. Trading options is a popular form of investment that is available to anyone, and it does not require large capital to begin. Spend some time and effort learning how to trade well you can make huge sums of money. This approach is called a buy and hold strategy. And this can help you increase your wealth in the long term.

When trading stocks, there are two ways of making money — a long position or taking a short position on a particular stock. If a share increases its value, then take a long position of buying the stock and sell the stock at a higher price. And if a stock reduces its value, then take a short position by selling the stock and later repurchasing it at a lower price.

Approaches Used in Swing Trading

As a swing trader, it's vital to have different strategies when swing trading. Playing on the upswing and downswing movement of your trades, which lasts from one day to a few weeks and even longer if the trade is doing great. A lot of trading's are on the daily charts and trading daily on candlestick charts. There are traders who use shorter time-frame charts to pick an entry and an exit, and other traders use the longer time-frame charts such as a week and a month assessing a longer-term sentiment of the investment.

There are different strategies in swing trading, and there isn't an exact way to go about it. Each trader has their different methods and strategies. Before deciding which approach is best for your investments, here are some of the swing trading strategies:

- **The Fibonacci Retracement**

This pattern is best in identifying the support and resistance level and the reversal levels of the charts. Shares retrace some trend percentage before reversing, and it plots the horizontal line of Fibonacci ratios of 23%, 38%, and 61% on the chart. Most traders also monitor the 50% level, although it does not fit the pattern, because the reversal of shares retracing half of the previous moves.

Traders can enter a shorter-term selling position when the downtrend price retraces and bounce off the retracement levels of 61.8%. And exiting the selling position for profit when there is a decrease in the price and bounce off the 23% line.

- **The Support and Resistance Trigger**

The trigger lines represent the basis of the technical

analysis that builds a successful strategy for a stock swing trading around them. The support level shows the price levels on the chart, which is below the price market, where the selling pressure is less than the buying. This results in the price decline, which is halted until the price turns up again. The trader enters a buy trade that has bounced off the support lines and putting a stop loss under the support line. Support is conflicting with the resistance. Resistance supports the price level above the current market, where selling pressure is higher than the buying pressure, resulting in low prices against an uptrend. In this case, the swing trader enters a selling position with the bounce off resistance levels and placing a stop loss on top of the resistance lines. The essential thing is to incorporate the technique, and they can switch roles – support can become resistance and the opposite way too.

- **The Channel Trading**

This is one of the swing trading strategies that need you to identify stocks that are displaying a stronger trend within a channel. Plotting a pathway around a bear trend in a chart, it's advisable to open a selling position when the price goes down the top line of the channel. And use a channel when swing trading, it's essential to trend trade, when the stock in the downtrend price, looking for a selling position except there is a break on the price of the channel increases showing a reversal and starting an uptrend.

- **The Ten-And Twenty-Day SMA**

This is a simplified approach used in swing trading that involves using Simple Moving Averages. This simplifies the price data by calculating the updated price average, which is taken in a range of specific time. The ten-day SMA will add up the closing prices daily for the ten days, dividing it by ten to get the new average for each day. The connection of the single standard creates a simple

line that assists in cutting out the sounds on the chart. The length used, and in this example, ten, you can apply to any interval from one minute to a week. SMA, with shorter periods, reacts faster to changes in price than other longer timeframe. In the ten-and twenty-day trading system, apply the two SMAs of measures to the chart. The ten-SMA cross above the twenty SMA buying signal is created to indicate an uptrend. If the ten-SMA cross below twenty-SMA, the selling sign is designed to show a downtrend.

- **MACD Crossover**

The simple way of identifying opportunities to swing-trade stocks in by using the MACD crossover swing trading system. This system is most famous as a swing trading indicator in determining trend directions and reversals. MACD is made up of two averages and MACD. When these two lines cross each other, a buying and selling signal is generated. A bullish trend is indicated when the line crosses above the signal line, and this is when you enter a buy trade. A bearish trend suggests a selling trade. When the two lines pass again, this signals trades in the opposite direction, and this is when the trader should exit a trade. MACD is around a zero line, and when MACD crosses above the zero lines, there is a trade signal indicating a buying signal and a selling signal when the zero lines are below.

The Right Market for Swing Trading

Both the bear markets or bull markets, swing trading, is different in a market with the two extremes. Both bull or bear market, you will carry the stocks for an extended time in a direction. This confirms that the best approach is trading on long-term direction trend.

The swing trader as an advantage when the market is not going anywhere when there is a rise of the indexes and a decline in the few days and again repeating the pattern. A few months later, with significant share indexes at a similar position as the first level, and the trader has various chances to find the shorter term, up and down movements in a channel. However, the swing trading limit is primarily on identifying accurately the market type experienced at that moment. You can use the Williams %R is a technical indicator to be able to get an idea when the market is at a short term extreme and if it's likely to reverse. This indicator calculates the close in relation to the range over a set time.

Some of the characteristics of these markets are:

- **Supply and Demand**

The demand is stronger, and there are weak securities in a bull market, many traders are buying, and very few traders are selling. And this increases the share price as many traders are competing. The bear market is the opposite of the reaction for the bull market, here many traders are selling, and less are buying; thus, there is a drop in the share price.

- **Psychology**

The perception of a trader towards market behavior can impact the market, and it can influence the rise or fall of the market. There is a mutual dependency between market performance and the investor's confidence. For example, the traders are eager to invest and make a profit in a bull market while in a bear market, traders are a bit negative, and they move their money in fixed income security. They ride the storm out and wait for a positive move.

- **Economic Activity**

The companies with stocks in the market exchange are also part of the economy, and they are linked to one another. A bear market means a weak economy, and most companies are not making huge profits since consumers are not spending a lot; thus, this affects the stock market value. A bull market means a strong economy, and companies are making huge profits, consumers are spending a lot, and this increases the stock market value. The best position for a swing trader when there is a stagnant market, indexes might rise for some days giving an overall trend. An experienced trader can take advantage of these movements to gains profits.

Chapter 2: Basic Concepts in Swing Trading

Swing Trading Strategy

In order to understand the swing-trading strategy, you will need to understand the basics. You need to know that when your target is around 25% profit from your stock, in actual sense, it is just like 5% to 10 % in the tough markets. Those are the type of profits that are considered life-changing, especially in the sought-after markets, basing your current time factor. As a swing trader, your goal should not just be on the gains that you anticipate over months or weeks, even though most of the trading period lasts around 10 days. You need to know that there are chances that you can make smaller wins that can accumulate to bigger wins. It is the same instance as having a profit of 20% in a month or around 5% each week; all matters in the period.

You will also need to factor in things like losses and risks; when you have smaller gains, they will be matched with your portfolio if the losses are also smaller. This is something critical since when the system is corrupted, the loss will end up affecting your smaller gains. When you are dealing with individual trades, you will be guaranteed to have larger gains. When you have a stock, it can show great strengths at the beginning for better gains and again making the remaining position to remain unpredictable.

There are different rules that help as strategies that can be used in swing trading. They are normally classified into two elements. The first one is that when you have a swing strategy that is working, then that is considered as entry filter. The common entry filter that is used is the Bollinger Bands. The second one is the price action method.

Step 1: You will need to wait for the stock price to reach the Bollinger Band upper level. The first element will apply here in a way that the simple strategy

is that you will have to wait and monitor the stock price and ensure that it moves into overbought territory. If you want the strategy to work, ensure that the first element is incorporated.

Step 2: The next step is to ensure that the stock price goes below the middle Bollinger bands. This means that the price needs to have touched the upper Bollinger band first and that there is a confirmation that there is activity in the overbought territory and that the current market will reverse.

Step 3: Ensure you use the swing-trading indicator. You need to have the breakout candle that is big enough to close at a low range and that it sells at the breakout candle. The best swing-trading indicator will predict the sell-off and then use the simplest method called the candlestick. When entering the market, you need to use the biggest bearish candle that will break below the Bollinger Band. For any swing trading strategy to work, ensure that you have simple entry filters.

Step 4: You will notice your gains when you break and then close back, ensure that you close over the middle Bollinger bands. This will most definitely work within a short trading period. You need to be worried when the breakeven is above the middle Bollinger banks; you will need to take your profits as it can signal a reversal. The main reason why the profit is taken is that it is an early signal that the stock market will rollover.

There are some strategies that can be complicated and confusing, that is the reason why you will need to adapt a simple strategy in swing trading, and this will end up guaranteeing success. The best strategy in swing trading should include a swing-trading indicator that can help in analyzing the financial structure.

Types of Stock Used in Swing Trading

When you decide to start trading, ensure that you pick stocks that are profitable. These will include:

✔ **Advanced Micro Devices (AMD)**

These are stocks that are considered to possess high beta, plenty of volumes, and they have the potential to earn more and higher in an uptrend. They normally trade below a dollar and as high as over $30. Their range is considered higher than their current price per share.

✔ **Nvidia**

This stock was announced after cryptocurrency in the booming time. This made its stock price drop to around $38 beginning of November 2018. Most of the analysts and officials have declared that the graphics have gone down and that it is now trading at 20%

✔   **KEMET Corporation**

They make electrical components like sensors, actuators, and capacitors. They have been in operation since 1919, and they have maintained a demand, and they have had better earnings.

✔   **Netflix and Amazon**

These are shares that are highly-priced per share, and their earnings are expected to be on the dominant trend.

What Stocks Are Good for Swing Trading?

Before choosing which stocks are the best, you need to know that swing trader is known to hold stock for a shorter time, and they will sell at a profit. The trick is to learn how you will buy stocks that have an upward movement and then start predicting your sales before the price drops. If you are new to swing trading, practice on how best to pick the right sticks for trading. You are advised to look for large-cap stocks; the main reason is that they exchange hands easily hence faster to buy or sell.

Look for stocks that are considered calm and those that do not have huge moves. Look for the stocks that have up and down movements with no drama. Remember, the main reason for swing trading is to make a living, not a killing. There are three shares that are considered easy to buy and sell, and they have a regular show. These stocks are known to make paper trades, then move to real trades and make real dollars and ensure that you learn the signals to buy or sell the stocks.

1. Facebook Inc.

These stocks are the best when it comes to learning new trend lines. When you at the stock chart, there will be zig-zag upward movements, and all the low points will line up in the pattern. You will be able to have the approximate lines across the low points that are what is considered the trend line. And anytime that stock level meets on that line, it will go back. What makes this stock the best to start with is that the bottom trend is already known. What you need to ensure is that the chart indicated a moving average at 50-day, this is what is considered the bottom trend line for this type of stock at the current time.

You also have the option to draw a line across the

areas that hit the stock.

This is because this type of trend will always reach an upper trend, then will drop down to the bottom line. The trend lines are considered approximate, and you will need to know when the price of the stock will turn around, instead of having a strict adherence to any trend lines that you have drawn. In recent times, the stock had a breakout that was above the upper trend line; they ignored the indicators and drew the trend line on the charts. It is believed that over 30 million shares are bought and sold each day, so this means that there are higher chances to buy and sell. What you need to make sure is that the stock is liquid, and you will not have an issue when the stock price drops.

2. Microsoft Corp.

You can trade these stocks in the same way you will do for Facebook stocks. On the lower trend line, these stocks also work on a 50-day moving average, and they will serve as a rough guide even though it will not be as neat as that of Facebook stocks. Their upper trend is considered ragged, so you can use this stock to learn about when a stock will rise or fall. The best thing is that the stock will trend regularly, and that will be enough to count on it, and it will help in learning the best time to buy and sell. You will need to draw a line on the highs to know of the right value for the selling price. You should know that the higher the trend line, the higher the chances that the line is accurate. There are records that over 30 million shares are bought and sold on a daily basis.

3. Apple Inc.

When you decide to settle for these stocks, ensure that you have more expertise as compared to Facebook and

Microsoft. This stock is known to always have an upward trend, but it is known to have formed new trends that can also change. This stock is known to be establishing itself, and you should know that these new stocks are considered unreliable and not established with solid grounds. This stock is the best when it comes to learning, their many products, announcements, and launches have many effects on the stock price. You will need to look for such announcements and know how they respond.

This stock brings about new and extra elements to swing trading. You will need to look for the technical indicators that are on the charts, and that can be combined with other strategies and fundamentals. They have so far sold and bought over 30 million shares on a daily basis.

It is advisable that when you decide to do

swing trading, you will need to choose a company that does well and has better, established patterns. Start by making your predictions and you will enjoy swing trading.

Is Swing Trading Better Than Day Trading?

When you decide to do your trading, you need to decide between swing trading and day trading. This can be a difficult decision. If you consider yourself a trader, then day trading and swing trading will be the same thing. Both trading's use the same approaches and methodologies, they are also all done under a short-term period depending on price fluctuations in the market.

To know if swing trading is better than day trading, you will need to know of the benefits of swing trading. Swing trading is known as a stock trading that traders use on a weekly or monthly basis as an investment. This is considered a medium-size investment because when one trades it will break or make it within 2-30days and that is the reason that the long-term investors will not be interested in trading in. Swing trading is known to combine two unique circumstances, the slow pace in investing and the rapid gains that fall under day trading.

Swing trading will be considered complete when you are able to analyze stock data. You will be able to know of any current stock that is rising quickly within a short time. The swing trader will buy the stock, then wait for it to increase its price and value and will move out of there is a market connect that will cause the price to drop. That is what is considered the trick to swing trading, you need to be clever and identify the trade and then get out after you get the maximum profit.

There are different benefits to swing trading:

• Swing trading is known to have a narrow focus, this because it is technical and based at looking for trend in a short time to help in increasing their values. The shorter period will help in focusing on the market situation and volatility and the current momentum. You will only need a short time to know of the market bias and when to trade. You do not need a variety of data like the company's financial records like balance sheets or other information in order to get the right knowledge to help in trading. The narrow focus is advantageous since it will help you to concentrate on the important areas and then become competent. In swing trading, the trick is knowing the stock price and the current trends. This is the main reason that swing trading is known to be less stressful compared to other short-term trading like day trading.

• With swing trading, you are able to know all your results quickly. As you know, swing trading involves trading for a few days to a maximum of a month. You will be able to know about your results after a short time even in a week's time. This will give you the ability to know about the new strategies and approaches to adapt and earn more money.

• Swing trading will help in generating your monthly income since there is no need to sit around and wait for months and years to start earning. Like the way most long-term investment has to do, you will know all about your earnings in the trades you have made and how much out of that to be considered an income. There is room to create more income by doing more trades weekly and they will be finished in less than two weeks.

- Since swing trading is done in a short time, there is the element of saving time. You will not need to have close monitoring when trading and hence the best investment to traders who do not have much time to trade. This is best for those who trade on a short-term basis while having a full-time job. When you are competent in technical analysis and based on the narrow focus on things, you will not need a lot of time to know of the key trends in order to trade.

- With swing trading, there is enough room for controlling risks. The main advantage of swing trading is the ability to minimize risks. This is because the trades are on a short-term basis as compared to the long-term trades. You have the option to place a large size of stock instead of the ones in low leverage like long-term trends. The other reason for low risks is that you are only making around 3 -5 trades weekly and hence no broad spectrum in investments. You will have close tracking of your trades and hence need for a short time.

The Classes of Assets

Most investors will ask, what is an asset class? This is a group of investments that have the same features and subject to the same laws and rules. There are three main asset classes, equities, bonds, and cash equivalent or commonly known as market instruments. The investment assets are categorized as intangible and tangible instruments. Investors will buy and sell in order to get income on a short-term or long-term basis. There are also alternatives to asset classes, like valuable inventory and real estate. Others include crowdsourcing, capital, and cryptocurrencies.

These assets are used in building an investment portfolio. The four categories are used together in order to avoid disaster and take advantage of the different strengths.

How Long Should a Swing Hold a STOCK

When trading, you need to be aware of the term settlement; this is the official transfer of security to another person. It normally takes a few days for the process to be completed. There is a 3-day rule when it comes to holding stocks when you buy your stocks the brokerage company is supposed to get the payment not later than three business days when the trade is executed.

And when you sell your stock, you need to deliver the stocks within three days to your brokers. The 3-day rule also deals with mutual funds, bonds, and securities. This rule is for investors who have stock certificates and have to physically be at

an event and the stocks that are traded
electronically.

Chapter 3: How to Start with Swing Trading

Swing trading refers to a trading strategy applied over a short period preferring for a sell or buy condition using trading indicators based on a forecast of a downward or upward trend over the next two weeks at most and one day the least.

By identifying a stock that seems to project high price mobility, traders are best set out to either sell or buy the shares. In this trading, the long-term value of a stock is usually left unturned. While swing trading seats between day and trend trading, Swing traders hold their shares for as long as three weeks to better identify the basis of a stock weekly or monthly through which choices are cornered by optimism and pessimism.

For a sweet pie, under swing trading, any corporate changes made within this period take time to show their market reactions, which would then mean string trading would already have maxed out to its technical ability. Like all trades, the most crucial part of this is picking up the most justified stock.

While Large-cap stocks switch from high extremes to low extremes in different directions, the swing traders trend maintains its course for a couple of days or months only to succumb to reverse off its direction when things change.

Under either market extremes of raging bull and bear market environments, swing trading still shows it is on a different league of challenges than just those available from the market of conflicting sides. Under high levels, at times, the most active stocks will be thought of as unusual as they lack similar up and downs oscillations compared to when identifications are stable for weeks or months.

A swing trader is most efficient as a tactic when market positions are not in a panic reaction to an external factor. When market identifiers rise for a few days then drop for a couple of days, we have a suitable routine to practice the swing trading. The major problem raised while trying to practice this method is that which faces long term trades too. The problem lies undeniably on the success of correctly identifying the market under experience.

How Much Capital Is Needed in Swing Trading?

The price to start on swing trading is usually set to zero. That means one could start making profits with as little as they possess. For day traders who are identified by their daily transactions and higher profits, they have to maintain an account balance of $ 25,000 under the laws of the united states. To avoid being categorized as that, then one would need to work a late-night schedule. Capital required to get it done will surely depend on position sizes, the intended account risk as well as trade risk.

A trader can also make the bold choice to decide on the trades to be so close to the margins whereby the leverage doubles, allowing for profits to be one hundred percent. The risk is always based on capital and rather not the amount.

Taking into account that all stock trading is risky, then someone can understand that even when placing stocks with a stop loss, it is still possible to lose all capital. For a trader that deposited capital but trades on leverage, then it is possible for them to lose more than the money. Risking at least one hundred dollars per trade is wise to avoid the significant losses under commissions as they become a bigger part of the capital as the trading capital is reduced. Commissions can usually be a major part of the loss or erode profit margins. Still, when taking more significant amounts, the commissions do tend to shrink in ratio to the profit, thus become less to worry about.

By use of unique parameters to better become an efficient trader under controlled capital, then one can understand that they require between $5 000 to $ 10,000 as a minimum to consider becoming a profitable swing trader on stocks. By risking two percent on each trade by the use of $100, then one can say that the trader requires a capital of $5,000 (0.02 x $5,000= $100). By deciding to lower the risk to a one percent per trade, a swing trader would require a minimum of $10, 000 (0.01x $10, 000= $100).

Through this tactic, it becomes possible for a swing trader to buy most stocks, including the expensive ones in the market share. Taking an account with $

5,000 in the capital, then a stock worth $ 200 is acquirable. The stop loss would be best suited to be $190 for every share. This adds to $10 being the trade risk on every share bought. Taking the swing trader is willing to risk up to $100 on this stock, then that amounts to a 2% stake of the capital. By risking ten dollars per share, then one is eligible to buy ten shares of the stock as ten shares x $10 = $100 that one is allowed to risk on.

Taking a swing trader that acquires ten shares at $200, then the total cost would amount to two thousand dollars. This being lesser than the capital in the account it would mean that the trader will have more space allowing him/ her to take in more trades and bigger count if the trader uses leveraging technology that allows for up to a ratio of 2: 1 which would be similar to a

$10,000 account of capital for every deposited $5, 000.

Lowered priced stocks would also work in the same strategic route. Taking a stock trade worth two dollars, then a comfortable stop loss for every stock would be placed at $1. 90, which would make the trade risk $0. 10. With the trader willing to risk one hundred dollars or even more given the principle that it is less than two percent of the capital account. Using the formula $ 100/ $ 0.10 = 1000 share position size. The position on this share would cost the trader two thousand dollars (2 dollars x 1000 shares), thus allowing for more room on the trading account.

In the above trades, the trade risks used are a mere five percent away from entry (a $10 trade risk on the first share and $0. 10 on the second share). This trade risk is considered adequate when using it on swing trades through stop loss is always considered to be affected based on the trading method and strategy. The minimum set on each strategic account is to avoid practicing under too much

risk on every trade placed as the least amount one can is predetermined due to huge commissions hurdle.

The risk of losing at least one hundred dollars on every trade is more advisable since a scenario should be placed in such a manner that the trader always takes more of winnings than the lose were it go turn south against predictions. Taking a stock risk of one hundred dollars, a trader would expect to make two hundred to three hundred dollars of profit margin. In some cases, the profit margins would still be higher. Were the trader to risk only ten dollars, then the profit margins would be in the region of twenty to thirty dollars while remembering most of these profits would be choked up by commissions. It explains why it is crucial for a trader to use a bigger chunk of his capital or leverage account on every stock. As the account grows, the trader is always willing to stake higher, and hopefully, with skill and experience starting to build up more positive results are obtained.

Given five thousand to ten thousand dollars is usually the minimum set for a swing trader, it is advised that one starts with a much higher capital balance to avoid being flag after minor or few losses. With a bigger account such as that with one hundred dollars, the risk of one percent or two percent, the rewards would compensate the swing trader and more than make up for it.

Can One Make Money Swing Trading?

The most efficient method to tell if one can make a profit under what capital is by use of a specified formula

Position size x the trade risk x (100%/ account risk%) = recommended capital investment

Taking a swing trader that places risks of one percent then buy a hundred share with the trade risk of two dollars using the formula

Two dollars x one hundred x one hundred = twenty thousand dollars. This shows the amount one is supposed to profit from the stock being successful. By initiating the leverage on the account, the swing investor then has at least twenty thousand dollars giving him/ her ten thousand dollars of the required amount to achieve that trade.

Be willing to take a 2% risk on the account under every trade; then, one would require a ten-thousand-dollar capital. As noticed, account risk and trade risk always determine the size or amount of the capital required. As expected, every stock is usually different from the other or next stock at any given time. It is better to account for these variations and use that when determining how much to deposit. Study stock charts over some time before deciding to enter, and as a guideline as to the best way, one can place a stop loss.

Waiting up until you have enough capital to engage in swing trading is considered a better tactic than getting in prematurely, which in most times than not warrants for losing the whole capital. In this case, being disciplined and the patient will, at most times, warrant better results than not. The strategies one uses will also matter a lot as they determine the success rate of an analyzed stock, which should be hired if done carefully. When swing trading, forex trading, or stocks, it really does not matter as all profits are similar in potential with the major difference being the amount of capital required to start a successful trading campaign on each market.

When swing trading forex, the price always moves in pips. When swing trading (based on a short time), a trader usually uses twenty to eighty pips for stop loss while watching out for the pair being traded. Under forex, the smallest possible position is a thousand worth of currency. On this a thousand worth of currency, a single pip movement is worth $ 0.10 for the Great British pound against the U.S dollar and the Euro currency against the U.S dollar, most commonly traded currency in the world. This thus means that for two thousand worth of currency, equates to two micro slots under forex trading; the trader is on the gamble of making or losing $ 0.20 per pip. The mini and standard lots are to make or lose a dollar to ten dollars for every pip of movement.

From such information, the expected profit can be estimated using a swing trading system. By risking 1% of a five-thousand-dollar stake, one can risk up to fifty dollars per trade. For a trade that uses a fifty pip stop loss and a one fifty pip target, it can be said that for each specific trade, one can secure ten thousand worth of currency. By losing fifty pips, one loses fifty dollars while by price reaching its target, one gets to make one fifty dollars. Having $5, 000 and leveraging it to acquire a $ 10, 000 since leverage helps one take multiple positions at a time.

Taking a monthly success rate of sixty percent, the reward risk on trades ends up being approximately 3: 1, which would mean a $ 3 gain for every dollar placed at risk.

Three positive trades worth 150 each give a total of $450, while for the two trades lost before account for $100, which would then suggest that every month, a total of $ 350 is gained. An advantage for most forex swing traders is that most brokers are commission-free. Most swing traders have a habit of compounding their accounts. This is whereby they withdraw some portion of the profits while leaving the rest in their accounts to maintain growth. A problem arises when a cap is reached whereby bigger potions of the profit are withdrawn and funneled to other investments. Through these traders attain their comfortable cap i.e., for a month or a year, then stick to that figure while avoiding growth in swing trading.

Compounding is not a bad idea; issues arise as income grows; thus, motivation reduces to lesser and lesser values. Most independent traders will aim to make their target returns on an amount or capital account they are most comfortable with. The most favorable route to take is to make sure your account gets profitable first, as that is the hardest part, getting the stone rolling.

No matter the type of trade, the profit outcome is affiliated with the account capital and commissions. With regular training and practice, one notices similarity within every specific market over a while. This does not suggest either market being superior just that each market behaves uniquely, such as to suggest personal preference.

By maintaining discipline and keeping wins over losses, one can make a good secondary resource while pushing for it to become the first income once success and account are big enough. It is expected for variations of incomes from month to month over time, ranging from below to higher of the personal average.

Allowing your mind to learn over a period of time is the best trading discipline you can achieve out there. Like other successful traders, most people begin out by failing. Practicing, reading, and taking advice for the first six months can help someone reach the top at their peak. After mastering, it becomes easier to analyze and prepare a trade. The time taken can even reduce by eighty percent from the initial once different methods evolve into sense over time.

Daily Routine of a Swing Trader

A daily swing trading involves the technical analysis and fundamental studies to provide a trader with price movements at perfect moments while avoiding the short or long idle times. This allows for the most efficient use of capital and provides higher returns as a reward if done right. Swing trading is difficult for actual retailers, while professional traders have more leverage over the market, provision of information, and lower commissions with the only limitation being the instruments of work.

A swing trader begins his/ her day well before the market opening bell to gather information of the day before price changes. This allows for a trader to predetermine the roots of any price variations that may happen.

Trading begins by catching up on as much latest news as possible and societal changes. This encompasses popular television channels alongside market sites. This can be divided into new acquisitions, legal turfs, and much more common, the overall market sentiment. The next step involves finding the appropriate potential trades. This is done by getting into trade interest through catalysts, which can include news, instincts, and information divergence from companies. Once interested in a trade, technical analysis is carried out.

Soon after, a trader is expected to make a watch list for trades to follow up on during the day; this gives trader time to observe the target prices, both target prices, and stop-loss lines, for placing a buy or sell order. The next logical step usually involves checking up the position of the stock while reviewing information to ensure no significant news exists out there about the stock.

The market hours will then be the chance

to buy stocks and stay keen for any
change.

After hour markets remain a time just to watch as
trades are already too much spread about,
the trader at this moment takes time to
check for open positions and determine
any material that can influence his/ her
holdings.

Chapter 4: Tips and Advice for Beginners

Tips to Be Successful in Swing Trading for a Beginner

Being successful in swing trading calls for a lot of successful measures that need to be familiarized and acted upon so as to bring the whole idea of success. Swing trading is so much lucrative, but that idea is not promised if you just lay back and trade. Remember that acquiring losses in trading is also an option that can bring you down so bad financially and can even affect your conscious. Let us venture into some of the major ways in which a novice in swing trading should consider when starting swing trading:

✔ **Good Stock Selection.**

Choosing your favorite kind of stock before you commence swing trading.

This will help you to focus on a particular kind of stock, observe its kind of trading moves and get to learn and master from every angle of various moves. Specialization in a particular kind of stock helps the trader to become an expert in that particular stock and get to retrieve the best from it and this, therefore, implies that large chunks of success will be pronounced during various trading activities.

✔ **Sticking with Your Reasonable Goals.**

Remember that failing to plan is always planning to fail. In every strategical move you intend to apply, always go by your set plans. Swing trading is commonly practiced frequently through several trading turns. During these periods, profits are made during the good days as well as bad losses during the bad days. Downfalls should not establish the ideas in your mind that your plan has been entirely wrong this whole trading period. These kinds of ideas will compel you to head to other ideas that may really turn to be bad news leading to trading failures hence losing large loads of capital and in the end resulting in a great financial breakdown. This should never occur because this may really tumble down a particular trader, especially for a particular kind of beginner.

Let us look at some of the elements that should be entailed in a particular trading plan so that the whole idea of trading activities can be termed to be successful:

- **A Specific Target.**

A target is a specific amount that the other traders are watching to occur during trading or the amount of price that is about to be executed in a particular trading activity.

- **A Particular Limit.**

This is the maximum value that a particular stock price can hit in the market during a particular trading activity. A limit aids so much in capital management to a particular trader in swing trading.

- **Stop Loss**

A stop-loss value is basically a specific order that closes a particular closing price of a particular trader. This helps to withdraw from a certain kind of risk and limit the number of losses that are likely to be incurred during a particular swing trading activity.

- **An Add-On Point**
-

✔ **Minimize the Rates of Losses.**

Just like profits happen frequently in swing trading, the number of losses is also made. This statement should not give you the comfort that it is so okay to make losses in each trading you get involved with. Learn to always tolerate low amounts of losses in various trading activities and appreciating the value of capital in trading.

✔ **Learn to Diversify.**

Diversifying exposes a particular kind of trader to grasp the basic overview of various kinds of securities that are normally involved in swing trading. This equips the trader to know the likely kind of securities that they can get involved within swing trading once their favorite kind of stock goes wrong in the market. This also gives the trader a hint to know where to start once bad occurrences happen in the market on the particular stock that they have been dealing with. However, this should not limit a particular trader in specializing in their particular trading stock and getting the right expertise skills that are greatly needed to make huge amounts of success in swing trading.

✔ **Bear Much Patience.**

Patience is one of the attributes that need to be highly implemented during swing trading. Patience is greatly needed in the situation where the trader is making tremendous amounts of losses at certain sing trading points. Remember that making losses are always been an option in trading, an activity that has never been popular with any kind of trader. The trader needs to learn at hos of her mistakes so as the capital value lost can be immediately compensated by the large chunks profit amounts that are about to be made.

Patience pays a huge amount of profits and great lessons in swing trading.

✔ Target Trading at the Beginning of Certain Trends.

The adage, early bird catches the worm is definitely a win in this kind of strategy. Trading at the beginning of trends gives a certain trader the chance to get exposed to various kinds of opportunities that are available in the market. Moreover, the commencing part in trading bears limited amounts of risks that the trader would be pretty much excited to evade. Due to all these, the trader is likely to experience large amounts of benefits, for instance, profits, which will eventually impact success in their trading activities.

✔ Keeping Records.

Maintaining records is one of the ways of collecting and getting to learn from every

kind of activity that has been experienced
so far in trading. Records on various
strategies that need to be implemented in
trading, rules, and engagements,
successful used tactical measures, and
lessons, are a great help as part of the
trading records. They help a particular
trader to stay structural and go by set
rules.

✔   **Trade with What You Can Afford to Lose.**

Since we discussed that acquiring is and
will always be part of the consequences
that are normally involved in trading.
Bearing this in mind will definitely
caution the trader on the safe ways of
handling capital in trading.
Capital is a very important element when
it comes to trading. During trading, try as
much as possible to avoid the loss of
several amounts of capital which can
easily lead to a great financial
breakdown.

✔ **Have That Winning Attitude.**

Tough times call for faith and the hope of being successful in trading at some point during the entire journey. A winning attitude in a certain trader enhances the trader the positivity that is so much necessary and greatly needed during various trading activities. A positive mind is most likely capable of impacting good ideas and progress in a particular kind of trader. Good ideas set in a specific trading strategy highlight the smart ways that a particular trader is likely to implement in various trading styles leading to great business success and benefits.

✔ **Studying the Various Trading Charts.**

Trading charts are normally the graphical representations in trading that highlights the actual status of the various trading activities that a particular trader is currently experiencing in the market. Trade charts can be used in laying various strategies that are greatly needed in swing trading. Examining various trading charts that are available gives the trader the idea of what may lead to trading success and trading failure. This is one of the tips that should be considered by mostly a novice kind of swing trader when he or she is trying to consider massive success impact at various swing trading activities.

✔ **Work on Your Best Time.**

Everyone has that moment of the day or probably day of the week that he or she feels much proactive and has the tendency to be much productive. If a trader is much comfortable swing trading at short time frames, then create awareness to that particular trader that his or her wish has just been granted. Working at a specific favorable period of time lightens the mood of the particular trader and makes him or her to achieve all the best in their trading activities.

✔ Long and Short Trades.

As a trader, always look for the long kind of trades during bullishness trading periods and also the short trades during times of bearishness trading times.

This hint will expose the trader to good rates of profits in the trading market.

✔ Limit the Number of Losses.

It is highly advised by the experienced trader that if things are not working out in swing trading always try to find your way out. A particular trader can be aware of this by depicting the status of the actual charts and patterns that represent the actual activities that are happening in the market and making a conclusion out of it. Bad times trading periods can lead to great amounts of losses that are experienced in the market and leading to a great downfall financially.

✔   Avoiding Risking with More Than 1% of the Trade Amounts.

This kind of tip calls for the small and reliable kind of tips that a trader should consider before engaging in swing trading. The trader is likely to experience good small amounts of profits gains and even a smaller amount of losses will be experienced that will less harshly impact financial breakdown to the trader in question.

✔   Invest in Your Education.

As a trader, getting educated frequently gives the trader a chance to ace in trading. That occurs because as the trader learns, he or she is equipped with the various fundamental strategies that are much successful in swing trading when implemented. The skills and knowledge that the trader equips during trading enable the trader to become an expert in swing trading at some point during their swing trading journey. Education makes the trader informed widely on swing trading, an event that is really beneficial in swing trading since the trader is now able to manage various kinds of risks that may tend to happen in their trading journey.

✔ **Grow Your Trading Community.**

Remember that two heads are better than one in every circumstance. Learning with your particular community on various trading fields enhances much easier understanding since ideas or overviews on various tech fields get to be highlighted and discussions held. Experts in various types of swing trading fields also get to come and work together to produce very viable trading results.

✔   **Implementing the Use of Trade Stimulators.**

Preparing for what is ahead is so essential in swing trading. The potential trader is able to try out what swing trading is actually about and the basic moves that are normally needed in swing trading. The trader is able to estimate too on the swing trading field that he or she is likely to venture into. He or she is likely to estimate the amount and the kinds of possible risks that are likely to be effected during swing trading. This will give the potential trader the urge to research the possible risks that are likely to be incurred and the possible remedies that can be implemented on the possible risks. Some kind of stimulators brings about paper trading that is highly encouraged to most of the novice kind of traders and potential traders in swing trading.

✔ **Start with the Lower Volumes of Trade.**

Establishing your trading foundation slowly is believed to be the best step to step process that leads to large successful events in swing trading. Smaller volumes used in trading tend to bear smaller amounts of risks that are likely to be involved during trading as compared to large volumes of trade. Lower volumes of trade used in short time frames during trading are believed to extract good amounts of profits in swing trading as compared to the kind of stock that

has been engaged in. Most experienced traders encourage most traders to start with the lowest volumes of trade amounts that will help them to acquire good amounts of profits to be experienced and reduce the number of risks that are likely to be associated in swing trading activities.

✔ **Proper Risk Management.**

Swing trading entails pretty much the number of risks that are normally experienced in the day to day swing trading activities in the present market. The trader ought to learn and master the different kinds of risks that are common in the swing trading market so that he or she can evade the possible disadvantages of being involved in various kinds of risks.

✔ **Search for Volatile Markets.**

A volatile market is the kind of market where the market prices keep changing drastically and unpredictably. A trader is highly encouraged to deal with the short-term market fluctuations, a situation where the market range is likely to be larger. A wider market range initiates large amounts of profits to be experienced in the market hence making the swing trading activities much successful.

✔ **Always Be Consistent.**

Being consistent as a trader is a great attribute that a trader should widely adopt before starting swing trading. Consistency helps the trader stick to his or her initial trading plan and go by its strategies. This helps the trader in the part of decision making and prevents the trader from being clouded by the market predictability judgment and ending up making wrong decisions that will be eventually depicted by the number of losses that have been made in the market. Remember that if you decide to deviate your trading plans

perhaps because of some gambling,
then the chances of heading to some
trading downfall becomes really
high.

✔ Get Advanced with the Market Phases.

Sometimes it is so necessary to keep up
with the available market trend so that
the particular can feel and be informed
on the actual status of the market. The
trader is also able to predict the market
mood, like, for instance, when the market
is bearish or bullish.

✔ The Entry and Exit Points.

It was discussed that before really
getting into trading as a beginner, the
trader should be familiarized with the
actual swing trading activities in the
market. During the practice, the trader
should be able to spot the factors that
trigger one to purchase and sell stock
shares in the market. Get familiar with

the actual activities that occur during the peak and the off-peak trading periods.

✔ Take Care of Your Made Profits.

The behavior of accumulating the made profits until they are is some great heap is termed to be so risky. It is advisable that the trader should take some portion of the made profits and secure them before entering the resistance level. After that has been achieved, the trader ought to exercise a stop loss amount to the deficit amounts of profits that have been left in the market.
Doing this exposes the trader to fewer risks in the market and secures the trader in a much better position.

✔ Hardworking and Determined.

Putting much effort in swing trading in terms of grasping the necessary

learning sources needed, examining, and
mastering the various swing trading tools
and much more always lead to great
success in trading.

Chapter 5: Tools and Technique used in Swing Trading

What Are the Best Stocks for Swing Trading?

The swing traders buy stocks for some days, and then they sell the stock for a profit. A new trader is also able to learn how to buy moving stocks and how to time the sales to know when to get out before the price drop back down.

For someone new to swing trading, the best approach is to quickly learn how to pick the right stocks to buy. Focus on large-cap stocks due to the numerous shares which can change hands at any given time; thus, they are quick to buy and sell. Calm stocks do not have huge moves. Stocks that slightly trend up and down with less drama. Don't focus on making a killing; focus more on making a living. Here are some best stocks that have distinct buy and sell signals. Follow these stocks and make paper trades, and when you gain experience, you can move to make real trades with real dollars and to learn signals for buying and selling.

- **Facebook**

This is the best share to learn to trade trend lines. This stock is suitable for new traders because the bottom trend lines are drawn for you, and the chart is showing 50-day moving averages. For the specific stock, it is the bottom trend line. Drawing trend lines across the upper side of stock hits. Facebook shares reach the high trend line, and it drops down to its bottom trend line.

These trend lines are similar and have the advantage of knowing the time the stock price will change instead of counting on strict instructions to the trend lines. For example, Facebook shares changes and moved the trend line on the upper side. Ignore the slide and draw higher trend lines using the next peaks on the chart. It's easy to find the buyers and sellers as nearly 33 million shares are sold and bought daily. You won't get stuck with stock since the stock is liquid, and you can sell when it drops.

- **Microsoft Corp.**

You can use the Microsoft shares the same as the Facebook stock. The rough guide for the lower trend line is the 50-day moving average; however, the guide is not used as the Facebook one. The upper trend line is a little split, and this makes the stock suitable for someone to learn and monitor when the stock rises and falls. The stock is regularly trending, and you can rely on it to follow this pattern for some time; however, you can study and monitor to time the buying and selling points daily by drawing lines across the upper to help you know the estimated value of the price to sell. The longer the trend is, the accurate the line will be. And nearly 30 million shares are traded daily basis.

- **Apple**

Apple Inc. shares require a little more expertise than Microsoft and Facebook. The stock has formed a new trend line, and the shares are trending upward. The trend lines can change at any time. The new trend can establish themselves but take caution, and the new trends are not reliable than developed stocks. Apple is the best stock for new traders on swing trading.

With product launches and news, this affects share prices. Stay clear on news announcements to see the stock response, and these can be valuable for your swing trading. Monitor the chart using the technical indicators on the chart and with the company's information and details to help you in trading.

Nearly 30 million shares are traded daily.

Best Indicator for Swing Trading

Thinking of venturing in the trading game? Getting the right technical indicators is an essential part. These indicators play a significant role in how you will understand trends and also the available opportunities when trading. In order to build a firm foundation, you will have to wisely choose the best indicators. Competition is tight, and if you choose poorly, predators are ready to take advantage of your earnings.

The first mistake new traders do is copying what other traders are doing, the following indicators that do not fit their trading screens. Gathering many indicators under their price bars, the wrong thing about this move is, it interferes with the signal production as it focuses on many angles at the same time. Indicators work by simplifying analysis and delivers the correct output on-trend, momentum, and timing. You can overcome this by having a different approach, research the information you want to focus on during that market time, such as the day, week, or month. Technical indicators can be categorized into five. Leading or lagging are the subcategories of these categorize. You can use the leading to predict the price movement, and lagging is used to report the conditions of the price movement.

As you begin, how can you make the right choice so as to avoid wasting your time on ineffective signal production? One of the most effective approaches is to start with the popular numbers and regulate one indicator at a time as you go. By doing this, you will be able to see the output if it is improving your performance or not. You will be able to know the exact needs of your levels by using this method.

You now know the five categories, let's go through each one of them to be able to know which one will suit you best:

- **Moving Average**

A lagging, this indicator analyses the movement of the market. The indicators are placed in the same panel in the price bars. Moving averages focus on the price action in a particular period, subdividing the total you find a running average for new bars. This focuses on identifying a trend, and The simple moving average is the best indicator to use. You should add all the closing prices for a particular number of days and dividing the total with the same number. If you use a graph, it will be possible to plot the average to better understand the market price.

- **Volume**

The volume is a measurement of how strong a trend is. When the price increases and also the volume signals, this means a stronger market. And an increase in price while there is a decrease in volume, this means a weaker market. If there is an increase in the volume, this means more people are confident in the trend. A decrease in the volume means people have less believe in the trend. A volume can be a trading indicator when swing trading, Volume can be used in swing trading to spot reversals and bullish signs.

- **Relative Strength Index**

The best explanation of Relative strength is buying when the indicator enters the oversold territory and selling it when it gets oversold. When a security is in an uptrend, this is when the signals are at overbought. And when security is at the downtrend, these signals are oversold. The swing trader should be able to determine the validity of the signals. Relative strength can be a mean reversion indicator and also as a momentum indicator.

- **Support and Resistance**

A simple explanation, these are price levels that security has trouble exceeding. When a security price falls to the support level, the increasing demand prevents the price from dropping any further. And when the security rises to the resistance level, the growing supply will prevent the security from gaining more. Both the levels are theoretical values formed on technical analysis. It's hard to break through a resistance level. And the old resistance becomes the new support level. A swing trader uses both of these levels to identify their entry or exit from a particular trade. An example is when a security has a $100 support level, it's essential to open long-term positions if the price is closer to that point.

- **Momentum**

This indicator monitors the rapid price changes. Momentum measures the speed of a specific market while picking natural turning points. When buying or selling signals go off, this means the histogram has reached its peak and its thrusting in the opposite direction via the zero lines. Various market data is generated when the height or depth of the histogram and the speed change interact.

How to Use the Best Indicators

- **Moving Average**

The use of moving averages is to define a trend and to recognize changes in the trend. Those are their only main uses; anything else will be a waste of time. A simple explanation is to a moving averages indicator is the total average price of a stock over a period of time. That's it; it's less complicated. There are two moving average used, the simple level and the exponential.

The simple level is the fastest one, while exponential moving is the slower one. It's best to use both of them. Why? Because when the faster one crosses, the slower ones, a trend change will be signaled.

There are some rules to follow when using the moving average:

- Pay attention to long positions only

when the sample is above the
exponential average and focus on short
positions only when the sample is
below the exponential. This is a
simplified rule to help you stay on the
right side of the trend.

• Remember that the moving
averages work mostly well when
there is trending share and not when
the trending range is noted. Moving
averages won't work if the market or
the stock is sloppy.

Important notes to remember, this applies
to long positions; however, you can
reverse for short positions.

- The simple moving average must be above the
  exponential
- There must be enough space between both the
  moving averages
- The two averages must be rising upward

- **Volume**

It's a measurement of the price of the financial asset traded in a given time period and the number of times the asset bought or sold in a specific period. It's often overlooked, but this indicator is a powerful tool. Information on volume is readily available, but not many investors don't have the knowledge of using this tool, and this is the reason why traders are unable to increase their profits and minimize their risks. There needs to be someone who sells shares to the buyers in the market, the same as there needs to be a buyer for a seller to sell his or her shares. A short-term price movement is created when the buyer and the seller battle for the best price in different time frames. You can boost your profits and reduce your risks if you use volume to help you analyze your stocks.

- **Relative Strength Index**

When you identify a trend, use the Relative Strength Index to capture sings in the overall trend. This indicator is commonly used to judge a market that is overbought or undersold. And it's represented on the chart from zero to 100. An overbought is when anything which is above 70 and anything below level 30 is considered an oversold. When you are in an uptrend, being out of the oversold territory may be a signal to buy. Having an overbought might signal an exit from the trade. While for a downtrend, moving out of an overbought might signal to enter a short trade. An oversold means exiting the short trade and not trading on the trend. Using these tools is pretty straightforward for trade selection. When you buy a stock, it should relative strength. When you want to buy a share between two companies, you can use the relative strength to be able to pick a stronger share. This is a tool used to filter the best stock to buy.

- **Support and Resistance**

Support is an area in which the asset price stops falling while the resistance is the point where the price stops rising. Traders need more information on those areas in a chart, as the definitions might not be enough. To effectively use this tool, first understand the asset price movement. There different levels of support and resistance; there is high and low. Higher levels are broke while major is likely to hold, leading to price movement in another direction. Minor levels are broken, an example is when there is a low trend, that low is a minor support. The price will eventually fall through that support level with no issue. This area usually provides analytical insights and any valuable trading opportunities. If the price drops below the minor, this means the downtrend is still solid. Major levels cause trend reversal. When the price is trending then reverses to downtrend, that point of transition is the healthy resistance level. And an area where the downtrend will end and the uptrend will begin is the strongest support level.

- **Momentum**

It is the rate of change in price security is called momentum. Momentum is an oscillator because the price cannot accelerate in one direction. When the price is on the uptrend, there is a definite trend, and when the price is on the downtrend, the indicator is negative. Momentum can also be the change in a company's revenues. When momentum is at an absolute extreme level, it is considered not suitable and can be used as a reversal indicator. When used in speculative assets, it might not function well. Momentum equates to buying or selling high or buying low and selling lower. The best time to make money using momentum is when the trade securities are moving the fastest.

Swing Trading Techniques

Trading is not rocket science, and there is no secret formula. The market can behave differently, and it might work with a specific strategy. And after some time, the market can change and shift to a new trading pattern, which can last for a shorter term or longer. So what works today might not work the following day. The main question is, what are the techniques you can use, which will work for a long time and can adapt to different market conditions? There are three techniques that can work best.

- **Breakout Trading**

The technique is to look for a new high

or low in the market. The high can be for some minutes or even for days. This technique focuses on using intra-day or daily time. This technique is best suitable for markets with lots of movement and good liquidity. A technique can work for years but can stop working due to market changes. An example, this technique has worked for over 8 years for a stock like Apple, but the stock stopped rising, and breakout was not able to work well with the stocks and the market.

- **Retracement Trading**

Retracement is also a commonly used technique when the market is moving fast in one direction, and it stops and corrects then begins a new leg of the direction the same way it was moving to. This technique is best for strong trending stock. The downside can lead to reversals, which make the stock to move further from the main trend. Few swing trading uses this technique.

- **Reversal Trading**

This technique is popular with swing traders since it offers a good risk to reward ratio.
The most essential is to have a method that has a good risk to reward ratio, and it works well with tough conditions where there is less market trending. The best method to choose is the one with high reward and low-risk profile. These technique does not work well with options trading; however, it works well with stock trading.

All these techniques depend on the market environment you are in.

Swing Charting

Swing trading is becoming a popular type of trading, and the technique used to recognize trends in the swing charting. In this chapter, we will look at how to use the charts to make a profit.

- **Importance of Swing Charting**

For better technical analysis, use the swing chart. This tool is widespread, and this is the reason why:

✔ You can simplify the process of locating trends by using this tool, and as you now know, the primary way to make a profit in the market is by using trends.

✔ This chart demonstrates less market noise; this way you can accurately other technical analysis that is not time-consuming.

✔ The swing charts show less market noise, helping you to be more alert and to apply other ways of technical analysis that aren't short term.

Different variations of the methods, for example, the Kagi, the Gann charts are very effective in locating trends. With this technique, you can make actual changes to help you improve your abilities in finding trends.

- **How to Use Swing Charting**

This can be used in various ways:

✔ Swing charting can be used to view a market trend. You can identify the patterns by looking for the highs and lows.

✔   You can use this technique to stop a loss and make a profit. And these trends can be applying in the moving stop-loss points.

✔   It can be applied to analysis that is not time scheduled. Fibonacci levels can be estimated, and you can use the Elliott waves. By doing this, you can monitor the shifting of prices.

✔   You can be able to create price channels by connecting the highs and lows. Thus helping you estimate the prices, profits, and stop-loss and liquidating positions at the right time. The price movement can be achieved by connecting highs to high lines and also connecting lows to lows.

Swing Trading Commandments

By gaining skills in technical analysis, you become more efficient, and this increases how profitable you will be in swing trading. There are many techniques available which a trader can use, but the most essential tool is the simple trendline. A swing trader can gain a lot of profit within a short time by using this tool.

By using these tactics when trading, you will have a winning swing trades. Here are some commandments of swing trading:

- **Align Your Trade with the Overall Direction of the Market**

Traders should make short-term trading decisions. The trends could hold themselves if the trade were successful for a short time since your focus was on the short-term stocks. However, you can pick the long-term trend and go with the flow and not against it. When having significant trends, there is the possibility of surprises such as upgrades and downgrades and hits and misses.

- **Enter the Trade at the Beginning of the Trend, Not near the End**

Quickly identify a pattern when it begins, you will assume less risk and add more profits. Noticing a change in trend can give you higher profits and fewer risks. By paying attention to the overall market averages, you will see when a trend is overbought or oversold and when it's prone to a reversal.

There are various indicators that can be used to monitor when the market is likely to a reversal. Industrial stocks are consistent with the overall market direction; thus they turn when the market shifts as well. Some of the early warning lights are indicators like candlestick and momentum, and they anticipate when stock will become. Crossovers and trendlines are the lagging indicators, and they only confirm messages of the early warning signs. You can choose to

trade with either lagging or a leading, depending on your willingness to risk.

- **Never Trade Only on the Short-Term Chart**

Synthesize the messages from the charts, use a two-year chart to analyze a stock. To monitor the long term moving average and the overall trend. Synthesize the complete analysis, and here you will be able to have information about the stock, is the stock breaking out? Is this information sufficient? Is adequate knowledge to be ready to trade in the short or long term to get a significant profit and fewer risks? Not all stocks you can be able to know the information clearly, such as the asymmetrical triangle are challenging to estimate.

- **Stay Consistent**

It is not easy to monitor all the stocks, and the more natural way is having a group of stocks that you will be tracking on a daily basis and learn about those stocks. Another tip is to focus on financial news, use the internet to browse various trading websites to check and analyze the upgrades, earning reports and any relevant trading information. You can also check the markets of other countries, the oil price, gold price, and the dollar trading. From the websites, you can check which stocks are active and save all the information collected. In addition, you can follow core groups of traders, pick a group with a broader sector, not just one specific group. And monitor their charts regularly and note their breakout levels, their stock prices, what they can make in a good trade and many more. Always stay alert, track several stocks, their portfolio, checking the charts regularly, staying updated with the latest financial news, and also analyzing the company's trading stocks. By doing this, you will be confident in making better trade winning decisions. With all the information, treat a

bad trade as an opportunity to learn more. Monitor your chart, stay to enter our trades early, set a stop-loss. The goal is being able to improve and get better as time goes.

Chapter 6: Best Strategies to Make Profit

How to Make Money Fast

Which are your money-making moves in swing trading? You need to have moves that enable efficient and fast means of earning money from swing trading. You need to select ways that are reliable for generating huge amounts of profit, with loss management strategies and also be able to protect your trading capital. Making money has always been a core objective for most traders who are much fascinated about this swing trading world. Below are some of the methods you can implement on your trading to make money fast in swing trading.

✔ **Aligning Your Trades According to the Market's Direction.**

Aligning trades with the market general's

direction can be a good strategy while you aim to get money fast through swing trading. This activity is highly recommended during the short-term kinds of swing trading as the trader is most likely able to stick with the actual market trends. The short- term trends are said to be really beneficial since the trader gets to learn new things in every trading activity. You are able to master the good moves, get to learn from their day to day activities and also have the chance of being exposed to various future opportunities.

✔ **Advanced Learning.**

Learning will always be part of every success of any type of trader. Learning enables growth and life immediately stops when we stop learning. Traders, mostly the ones new to swing trading, are highly advised to stick to this strategy. The advanced learning can be practiced by doing much research and staying updated with the news feeds. Doing more research on trusted sources online will make your knowledge in swing trading to widen and you well aware of all the basics that are needed for swing trading.

Have the desire to learn a lot and you will be aware of all the tricks and tips about swing trading. Also, it can be by joining educational forums online which hold discussions about swing trading. Learning from your mistakes and those made by other people will make you grow. They will make so cautious when you are handling your trades. Learning will save you from all kinds of con people online and you will be aware of even the steps of generating huge money with minimum risks and losses in swing trading. This can be done by getting engaged in most of the short-term trading activities.

✔ Short Term Trading.

Short term trading simply implies getting engaged in trading in short time frames. The short time frames in swing trading usually last for just a short period of time rather the entire whole day. They are highly encouraged because the chances of acquiring good amounts of profits during those particular days are so high. The rates of profits likely to be experienced in various short trading time frames are usually 5-10% rates.

✔ A Stable Trading Plan.

A trading plan is advised to be formulated at the beginning of your swing trading. A trading plan consists of your strategies and goals of your trading. If you want to have an efficient schedule for your swing trading, get yourself a trading plan. A particular trader ought to stick and be ruled by his or her initial plan and following all the respective strategies that are highly needed

in swing trading for it to be greatly successful. Be consistent with what is in store in the plan and implement every strategy in their respective kinds of trading fields. This will definitely prevent a particular trader from being compelled to decide while comparing it with what is happening in the market. A trading plan promoted discipline and responsibility in your trading and you are even able to monitor your swing trading performance.

✔ **Being a Structural Trader.**

Being structural implies that you are able to work out your things in a structural way and handle out things with a definite kind of attitude. This calls for the particular trader to always stay glued to their trading plan and never get compelled by the actual market happenings despite the largely influenced occurrences that tend to occur multiple times in the market. Be consistent with what you have planned out and always do all these with a lot of positive energy and positive aftermath will definitely follow.

✔ Selecting the Right Kind of Stock

Swing trading entails various kinds of stock that are available in the market. Different traders have different tastes on the type of stock they prefer for their trading. The potential trader is obliged to select the specific kind of stock that he or she is considering to work on in the market and correctly manage it in a way. This will definitely make the trader feel much comfortable with what he or she is working on and be able to come up with good expectations like the large loads of profits hence leading to great business success.

A trader is advised to select a type of stock that enables the generation of good profit since different types of stock are affected differently by the price fluctuations and the volatility in the market. Select a stock that is less volatile since it has less potential for the risks in the market. Do not choose a stock that will stress you a lot in the real market. Select a type of stock that you can handle and the one with fewer risks and low potential for losses in the swing trading market.

✔ **Goals and Targets.**

Do you really need to set goals for your type of trading? If you want to make good money fast in swing trading, all you need to have is a detailed set of goals. Realistic and clear goals are advised to be formulated when you are starting off with your trading. You need something like a bucket list to work on when you enter the swing trading arena. The specific goals and targets set by a particular trader are a big thing when commencing swing trading. They are the ones that guide a trader on the specific traces that an active trader should master and follow each and every time they get engaged in swing trading. Targets and goals are normally set so high by a particular trader so that they can act as a motivating tool in various swing trading activities in the market.

Higher amounts of profits are a common goal for most of the swing trading. Bearing what is needed at the end goal always motivates the trader to tackle the market moves with much intelligence and leads to the production of good results; large chunks of profits to the trading business. This strategy by a particular trader when he or she wishes to make money quite faster since a leakage about what is expected is already entailed in a certain trading plan that contains the targets and the respective goals.

✔ **Being Decisive.**

The actions implemented on all types of trading are normally based on the type of decisions you make. The better the decision the better the performance of your trading. Do not be afraid to sit down with an open mind and make the right decisions. Why make rushing and poor decisions that will not bring positive results on your trading? If you want to make good money, relax your mind, and make clear and strong decisions for your swing trading.

The ability of a particular trader to bear solid decisions when trading in swing trading markets is super important. If a particular action has been planned to be undertaken then it really needs to be followed during the actual trading.

The idea of selecting unsure trades while making decisions should not be considered at all. Unsure decisions made in swing trading lead to total failure. You can also consult experts in swing trading in the matters you are facing in order for you get help. It is also advised to have a master's in your swing trading who will be like a mentor to you and will also assist in evaluating the kind of decisions you have come up with.

How to Make Money Online

✔ **Do Not Make Any Changes to the Learning Curve.**

Alterations to the learning curve are highly discouraged at any point during the entire trading journey. Riding the learning curve by activities in the market should not be considered unless you want to ruin your way of working in the swing trading market. This will initiate much confusion when trying to implement the original trading strategies set and the updated and new strategies. If you feel that some key points have been left out in the strategy then try to consult various swing traders' experts. All in all, stick to what you have been wanting so bad for quite a while.

✔   **Well Utilizing the Demo Accounts.**

What are the demo accounts? Demo accounts are the mock accounts that are used by potential swing traders in the market when starting off their swing trading. Demo accounts are provided by different swing trading brokers on their trading platforms. You are advised to select trading platforms with demo accounts integrated with them. These accounts are normally featured with virtual money for the newbies to practice on their skills. The advantage of using such accounts is that there are no real losses incurred in the trading. Everything is virtual. This enables the novice traders to get the idea of what is actually happening in the market and they also get the chance to get the experience of how a swing trading market operates in its day to day operations.

Traders are able to perfect their skills before getting into the real world of swing trading. This will also expose the traders to the kinds of risks that are likely to happen in the market and getting the various good remedies of handling them. This also exposes the particular trader to the popular kind of mistakes that are normally made by most traders during swing trading and they get to master the possible solutions to be implemented to the possible problems in the day to day trading activities in the market.

✔ **Doing Blogging.**

You can decide to start off a blogging site about a swing trading topic to help passionate readers who love swing trading. You can provide guidelines on the various ways of being successful in swing trading. You need to be passionate about swing trading first in order to attract more readers to your blog. Blogging will generate income for you by means of selling products to readers and also subscriptions from the readers. You will, however, need to be patient with yourself since it takes times time before you start earning from blogging sites. All you need is much effort and persistence and everything will work out well. You also need to do much research when you are doing your blogging for wider knowledge in swing trading. This will enable your readers to be so informed and will get tips from swing trading.

Ways to Increase Profit

Profit maximization is always the objective of any kind type of trading. Below are various detailed points on how to increase your profit in swing trading.

✔ Finding the Trading Style That Totally Suits You.

There exist different styles of how to do your swing trading. You do not need to apply all the styles in your trading. Select the trading that you most prefer. Choosing the way in which you feel is much comfortable and where you likely to produce viable results should is so important in trading. Once a potential trader has spotted his or her favorable trading style, he or she is obligated to do some in-depth research on what the style actually entails and get the basic overview of how the cards are normally played on that side.

This kind of structural motive will eventually enable the trader to receive large loads of profits.

✔ **Shorter Trading Time Frames.**

Short term frames in swing trading are mostly advised in swing trading. The time frame basically describes the period of active time that a particular trader spends on swing trading during various occurrences. Shorter time frames are believed to be much profitable and much reliable for profit making during swing trading. Moreover, short time frames in swing trading experience a low amount of risks in the day to day activities as compared to the long-time frames. Do not select the time frames that will be tough for you to handle.

✔ **Good Trading Plans.**

Planning should be the first step any potential trader should engage in before commencing in any activity in swing trading. Swing trading plans entail the respective working strategies that a potential trader is required to examine and then master the basic points that are needed for the trading to be successful. Trading plans really need to be strictly followed and implemented correctly for trading success to be depicted through the amounts of profits that are about to be made in the end. Trading plans make your work easier and enable efficient swing trading. Lacking a trading plan is obvious preparing yourself to incur bigger losses in your swing trading.

✔ **Good Money Calls for Great Patience.**

What's all with the rush? Good things take time. In our case, the good thing is good money. Trading does not succeed in one day, it takes a reasonable amount of time. Calm down, everything will be alright. You will also gain a good amount of money with time. You need to do the right thing and you will eventually generate good money with time. Do not be in a hurry to rushing everything up. You do not need to stake all the income you have for your trading, you will lose everything. Use the right amount of our disposable income for placing trades. The higher the amount of money you offer for trading the higher the risks expected to rise. Try by all means to eliminate risks and losses in your swing trading to protect your trading capital.

Do not joke around with money allocated for school fees or for utility bills. Much sitting and getting to learn the various trade moves via the market trends, trading charts and other multiple learning sources promotes knowledge enhancement to the particular trader. The trader gets informed of what is actually happening in the market and what is entirely expected so as to achieve greatness in swing trading and receive large amounts of profits during various trading activities.

✔ Being an Active Trader in Part of Improvement.

Improving a particular field means that you are learning and generally growing as a person. A trader has to keep learning and getting familiarized with the actual market happenings that are taking place in the market. He or she has to know the kind of risks that are dominant in the swing trading market and the various ways of eradicating it and avoiding such risks from occurring in the market.

Chapter 7: Swing Trading Rules

Simple Rules of Swing Trading

Rules are always there to help you be disciplined in what you are doing. Have you ever come across the swing trading rules before starting on trading? This chapter is all about covering the different rules of swing trading. The rules will guide you on the best ways on how to yield huge profits and incur minimum losses from swing trading. Below are some of the rules that will help you in your swing trading.

Simple Rules of Swing Trading

✔ **Select Volatile Markets.**

There are different markets in swing trading. To be successful in swing trading and be able to earn huge profits, you ought to choose a market with wider price fluctuations as compared to the narrower ones.

✔ **Consider Consistency.**

Consistency is the key to swing trading. You need to have a swing trading routine and always stick to it. Be consistent in what you are doing to prevent confusion and messing everything up. You ought to do much practice on the swing trading market to be familiar with all tips and tricks to be implemented. Practice this with the mock accounts you are provided with by the different brokers.

Mock accounts perfect your skills by providing virtual money to trade with. Be consistent with this practice before entering the real swing trading. Real trading in the swing market is all full of risks so you need to be fully prepared before making up your mind to start off.

✔ **Be Aware of Market Situations.**

A swing trading market has different situations. The market can either be bullish or bearish. You need to be aware of the market you are dealing with. Bearish markets are normally weak as compared to bullish markets. Be aware of the situation you are in the market so that you are able to make proper estimates of your profits and losses.

✔ **Do Not Take Chances.**

Do not be in the rush of making good money within a short period. Good things take time. Do not associate yourself in swing trading with gambling. You will lose a lot. Have patience with the money you are receiving, and with time, the money will of course increase. Do not utilize the chances since they will make you lose all the money that you worked hard for.

✔ **Accumulate Profits.**

Making a profit is always the main objective of any kind of business. You need to have a way of handling your profits made in swing trading. Profits need to be accumulated using different market strategies to prevent losses. The different market strategies may include implementing stop-loss orders on the stock when it reaches its resistance levels.

✔ **Be Aware of the Support and Level of Resistance.**

Support and the level of resistance are very crucial in swing trading. The stock in the swing trading market needs to be monitored. You need to be aware of its support and the level of resistance. The level of support and resistance on the stock are the prices on the trading chart at which a trader is able to tell if you have more buyers than sellers. The two factors aid to control the number of losses in the market.

✔ Set Your Entry and Exit Points.

Having an entry and exit plans in swing trading are very crucial. Sometimes the market behavior may not be as favorable as you accepted. Things and activities may go in vain. You need to have a plan to escape from this when it happens. Exit and entry point now come in handy. You are able to know how to work things out when the market is in its worst-case scenario. Always ensure to enter into the swing trading market with entry or exit plans to shun from making huge losses.

✔ Take Advantage of the Stop-Loss Strategy.

This is the kind of swing trading strategy that makes you be able to exit your position in the market. Stop-loss order when buying the stock is normally implemented at a position which allows a little change in the price fluctuations but becomes unfavorable when the market gets out of control.

Most swing traders purchasing stock use stop-loss when the price of the stock drops on the market. Contrarily, when selling stock in the swing trading market, a stop-loss order can be implemented when there is a rise in the price of the stock since this is the resistance level of the underlying stock.

✔ **Minimize Losses.**

Losses are normally part of the game, but you need to do something when they become out of control. Losses affect your profits and your trading capital. You need to have some various working strategies on how to get rid of the losses in swing trading. Always implement the strategies when trading to succeed. If things are not working out well as expected, you need to quit what you are doing and work on something else.

Losses can make you lose a lot of money if you are not cautious while trading. The objectives of swing trading are all about raising profits and making investments and not making losses.

✔ **Have Control of Your Emotions.**

Do you know that emotions have made many traders fail in their trading? Emotions should not be part of any trader in the swing trading. Swing trading markets have both best-case and worst-case scenarios. You need to control your emotions when both scenarios happen in the market. You do not need to get over-excited when the market goes according to your favor. You need to be always alert not to drop tremendously.

Also, during your worst-case scenarios, do not get carried away with your emotions. Be strong and stop with the crying. When things do not work out as you expected, find alternative actions

immediately to be implemented in the
market to avoid huge losses and risks
in the swing trading market.

Do not feel bad when the mistakes
happen in your trading, they are normally
part of being successful in swing trading.
Learn from the previous mistakes made
to avoid repeating the mistakes next time
you are trading. Mistakes normally make
you grow and you learn a lot.

✔ Have a Trading Plan.

Who starts off something without a plan?
You need to have a plan for everything.
Swing trading requires a plan too. A
trading plan guides you in all your
activities. You are able to know the
actions to be implemented in different
market situations. A trading plan
provides you with the desired market
strategies and also assist in raising a
reasonable amount of capital. A trading
plan provides a routine for you and helps

you become disciplined when you are trading.

A trading plan creates a schedule for your trading, in terms of the time and the type of trading you are dealing with. Also, a plan also enables you to come up with the goals and objectives of your trading. Objectives help you put much effort so as to achieve the goals. Do not enter into the swing trading market without a plan, it is a crucial factor that needs to be integrated with your trading.

✔ **Enjoy Swing Trading.**

Why does something you do not enjoy? Swing trading requires much passion when practicing it. You need to be love spending much of your time on your computer since most of the swing trading markets are online platforms. You need to be excited when trading. This will motivate you to learn more about it and you will get much informed. Knowledge is powerful since it leads to success.

Do your trading with all the passion and enjoy it. You can also join forums with swing traders' experts to learn and see what others are doing. Swing trading is not an easy thing, you need to have much love and passion for it to succeed. A bored swing trader gets tired with time and decides to give up with trading. Be the happy trader and success will definitely come your way.

✔ Come up with Good Swing Trading Decisions.

The kind of decisions you make in trading defines you a lot. Do you expect success when you come up with poor decisions? A swing trader needs to make strong and good decisions while trading. You need to prepare yourself so well mentally on the best thing to do when the different market situations occur.

Do not be the kind of trader who makes poor and rushing decisions when things fall apart. Be a good decision-maker for better success in the future. Also, do not rely so much on what people are saying online. You need to come up with your own decisions for your own trading. Others may mislead you and this might make you fail terribly. Be strong and do the right thing.

Chapter 8: Money Management

What Is Money Management?

This term is used to refer to the process of investing, spending, saving, and budgeting; it is also used to refer to the way capital is used for personal or group usage. The other words used for money management includes portfolio and investment management. When you are good with money, it involves a lot apart from just meeting your needs. When it comes to money management, having math skills is not mandatory, there are different skills needed that will be discussed later.

Money management is simply how you handle all the finances and how you handle all your long-term goals. It also involves how an individual manages their investment in order to make great profits. Most people think that great money management skills are all about saying no when you are tempted to make a purchase. What it really implies is when you are able to say yes to what is important to purchase. When you do not practice good money management skills, whatever money you have might look little for your lifestyle.

To have a good start when it comes to money management, you need to know where you are. This is in terms of your financial capability and power; like assets and liabilities. Assets include your investment and bank accounts, any properties and retirement accounts. Liabilities are the things that you need to pay like credit card balances, any loans like student loans and car loans and any mortgages and outstanding debts. Your net worth is when the value of your assets is more than your liabilities. And when your liabilities are more than your asset that is considered a net loss or negative net worth. When you have great money management skills and approaches, getting a net worth will be easy.

Ensure that you set your goals in order to achieve great money management. Your goals will create a plan on how you will manage your money. When you have your goals set, it will give clarity on which are priority expenses and which you can let go. You will need discipline and effort in order to achieve all your efforts. For instance, when you plan to buy a car worth $20k, you will need to work harder and smarter and reduce your expenses. You will need to do all that as compared to someone whose budget car is $10k.

When you have your budget drafted and set, remember to have adjustments. When you prepare a budget, you have the chance to know all the expenses that you have. For instance, you can set aside $150 that can be for entertainment and any miscellaneous expenses after payment of all expenses and managing your debts. Good advice is when you get a pay increment, do not use the additional income for your entertainment but add it into your savings.

When you have a target to meet different goals, you are likely to have the money in different multiple accounts. A good example will be to ensure that you have a separate emergency fund so as not to get tempted for any impulse buying in the future. You will also have different strategies and that will be for different goals. You will be aggressive when you start investing in different stocks that you will not need to invest money in like 20 years. You need to also have an account that has no risks like a savings account that that can be used as emergency funds when the need arises. When you have such multiple accounts, you can use a software program to help in tracking the several accounts. A good one can be Quicken; it will track all your expenses and the savings goals.

The Basics of Money Management

Money management is a term that deals with solutions and services that are in the investment field. The good thing is, in the financial market there are different resources available that can help in personal financial management. For any investor, their intention is to have a good net worth, so it will come a time when they will need the services of professionals like financial advisors. The advisors are known to offer brokerage services, money management plans, and private banking. The advice is best for retirement, estate planning and other benefits.

When you are in business, it seems complicated when there is a need to manage cash flow and different accounts.

When you are able to strike a balance, you are guaranteed to be successful. If you are not able to manage all that, you will need to get the services of an accountant or bookkeeper to do all that for you. Even if you will outsource, you need to know the basics of money management and bookkeeping. You will need to know simple tasks like interpreting bank statements, understanding accounts payable and receivable, credit, and tax forms.

Money management will also involve knowing more about debit cards, checks, online payments, cash, and credit cards when it comes to payment options in your business. You will also need to have a planned and established payment plan and a debt collection system just in case of non- payment.

Opening a bank account is another way to help in money management, you need to choose a name and have an operating and registered business. Make sure you get more information on credit card facilities, a debit account, and any other additional services. Another important concept is to ensure that you have extended credit facilities in case of late payments. This can be planned for 30-6-90-120 days after a product is delivered or a service is rendered. You can motivate your customers to pay on time by extending discounts. Before the credit extension, ensure that you have done proper background check especially with large amounts. Even when there is credit extension, there are times where you will end up not being paid or not aid in time. To be able to recover your money, you need to ensure there is open and clear communication.

What Are Money Management Skills?

Before you can know of the best skills for money management, you will need to ask yourself some questions. What is your weekly or monthly income? Do you have a list of expenses that you need to pay? What you need to know is that money management is a skill used in life and cannot be taught in school. These skills cannot be learned in school but mostly from life experience.

✔ Have the ability to set a budget. This will help in tracking your expenses and the way you spend money. What do you spend a lot on, is it entertainment, clothes, or food? What is the tendency of overdrawing money from your bank account? If all that is yes, then you will need to set a budget. Look at your monthly statement and write down all the expenses in categories. You will be surprised by how much you are wasting.

✔   Spend what you have wisely. Always have a shopping list when you go shopping. Do you have a habit of looking at the product prices before putting it in the shopping basket? If you have coupons, ensure you use them. There are mobile apps and online resources that can help in focusing on your expenses. Do you know how to monitor your expenses? When you are not attentive to this advice, you will end up losing your hard- earned money.

✔   Always balance your books, do not always have a tendency of getting your bank balance online. When you depend on online information, there will be an issue when you want to know the balance on what you are spending at that particular moment.

Be accountable and ensure you record all your expenses and this will help in avoiding any over-spending.

✔ Set a plan that will help in accomplishing anything that you put your mind. When you have a financial plan, you will be able to track how you are spending your money.

✔ Always think like an investor. When in school, you will not be taught how to handle money but largely on how to invest your money and have wealth growth. Learn to grow your savings and to invest at an early age. Turn that $100 to $200, $400, $800, and more. Having a stable financial future means that you have invested and grown in your money. When you start thinking like an investor, your money will grow. If you have a spouse or partner ensure that, they also know about your financial goals. If you possess a joint account with your partner or spouse, always work together and agree on the financial goals. When you are stuck or in doubt, consult a financial adviser and learn a lot of how to invest.

✔   Save your money, always be focused, and committed when it comes to saving money and this will guarantee a better future. This will help in improving your financial positi0n and even make it better. The first step is to have the decision to do that and this will help improve your management skills.

Importance of Money Management

Money management will help any individual in living on a budget and within their means. You will be able to look for great bargains and avoid any deals you believe that is not good when making a purchase. When you start getting a stable income, you will need to know how to invest because that will help in attaining your goals. And when you practice proper money management, you will meet all your goals and plans. There is the importance of money management:

✔ You will have better financial security: When you are careful with your expenses and savings, you will end up having enough for your future.

Your savings will help in giving the proper financial security and you will be able to take care of yourself in case of emergencies. With your savings, you will not need to use your credit card in case of any issues.

✔ When you have proper money management and manage to save, you will be able to get opportunities and invest in the business. It will be frustrating to know of a great opportunity and not having enough funds to invest.

✔ Your credit scores will be determined by the way you manage your money. When you have high credit, score means you have managed to pay your bills on time and you have low-level debt. A high credit score means you will have more savings and you will be charged low interest when making purchases like cars or mortgages.

✔ Money management helps in reducing stress, this will happen when you start paying your bills on time. When you are late in paying your bills, you will encounter stress. Stress will bring about health problems like insomnia, migraines, and hypertension. You need to be aware of how you will handle money management, this will help in having extra cash and manage to save and manage a stress-free life.

✔ Money management helps in earning more money and when your income increases, you need to develop proper budgeting. And know of the right places to invest the extra money you have made. You need to know of additional venues to save money like in stocks and mutual funds; this will help in earning more money unlike

money laying in your savings account.
Ensure you learn about the
investments, not all investments are
profitable. The better thing about
investments is that you can be on a
monthly salary and still earning from
your investment.

✔   When you adapt great money
management skills, you will not
waste money on unnecessary things.
When you do not know how you are
spending your income, it will be easy
to be in debt. When you use your
spare time effectively, it will help in
managing your money. For instance,
when you spend time with your
friends and family members, ensure
that you are aware of your budget.
Peace of mind is guaranteed when you have
better money management
skills. When you a stable income and
better savings, you will be able to
handle any financial issues with

confidence that all your needs can be handled perfectly.

World Top Money Managers

These managers are known to offer management and investment advice. They manage both active and passive funds.

✔ The Vanguard Group: It is a well-known management and investment firm, they have more than 20 million clients and in more than 100 countries. They started in Pennsylvania in the '70s and they have grown their assets to more than $5 trillion by close of 2018. They hold over 300 funds, move 150 in the US and more than 400 indexes to all of their market funds.

✔ Pacific Investment Management Company: This management firm has

a worldwide presence and founded in
California in the '70s. They have
grown their asset base to more than $1
trillion by close of 2018. They have
over 700 professional managing
investments and with over 10 years as
experts. They have over 100 funds and
they lead in the fixed income sector.

✔ BlackRock, Inc: They started with
their main company as BlackRock
Group, by 1988 they started another
division and labeled it BlackRock,
Inc. They grew their assets to over
$15 billion in 5 years and by the end
of 2018, they grew to over $6 trillion
and they have become the largest
company in investment management
in the world. They have over 100k in
their workforce and over 50 offices in
more than 30 countries. More than
20% of their assets are equivalent to
$16 trillion.

✔ Fidelity Investments: This firm was founded in the '40s and by end of 2019 their customers have grown to over 20 million and more than $5 trillion in asset base. Their mutual fund is more than 300, this includes domestic and foreign equity, money market, fixed income, money markets and allocation of funds.

✔ Invesco Ltd: This firm has been in business since 1940 in offering investment advice. They announced in 2018, that they have made over
$800 billion way above their products. They have over 100 EFTs that are made from their share capital. In 2017, they had a decline and it affected their stock price. They have managed to be among the best in the world despite all the challenges and

setbacks. They have become among the top and best companies in the world, in terms of money, assets, and investment management.

The Approaches Used in Money Management

Great financial skills make money management easier, and how our money is spent largely affects your credit score and your debt cycle. There are tips that can help you if you are struggling with how to manage your money.

✔ Always have a Budget: Most people do not like to have a budget because they believe it is a boring and repetitive process. That involves listing all their expenses, summing up numbers, getting everything up, and running. When you have a budget, there is less room to be bad with money. You will get to know your income and expenses. The secret is focusing on the value that the budget will bring to your life instead of the budget creation process.

✔ After making the budget, the trick is to make sure that you use your budget. It will be a waste of time when you draft a budget and you do not stick to it. If it is a weekly or monthly budget, ensure that you refer to it often, and it will help when making your spending decisions. The budget should be made in a way that, at any given time you can easily track how much you have spent and know of any penning expenses.

✔ When drafting your budget, have a limit set for any unbudgeted expenses. In any budget, what is important to know is the funds left after paying all your expenses. When you have any budget and everything is settled, you can have the balance for your entertainment purposes. The amount set for fun should be a specific amount from your income. If you are planning to have a big purchase, refer to your budget first.

✔ Start by tracking your spending habits. When you have small purchases

they will end up piling and finally, you will notice that you have gone beyond your budget. When you track your spending plans. you will be able to know the places that you are failing and how you can rectify them. If you can, ensure that you save all your receipts and have a record of your spending in a journal. Have them in categories so that you can easily track them and know of the areas that are hard to stick on a budget.

✔   When your income is steady and qualifies you for a credit facility that does not mean that you should get that facility. You do not need to commit yourself to any monthly recurring bill. Most people think that the bank will not approve of the facility because they cannot afford it. What the bank knows is just your income exactly as you have reported. And if you have given a credit report, they will use what is offered on that report and they will not have any obligations not to give the credit facility. It is a personal decision to know if you qualify for the credit facility and if you have the capability to pay regarding your monthly income and other obligations.

✔   When making a purchase decision, ensure that you are paying the right and best prices. The best way to do this is by making a comparison and making sure that you are paying the lowest prices for the products and any services rendered. Look for discounts, cheaper alternatives, and coupons.

✔ In situations whereby you are planning to make a huge purchase, ensure that you save for that purchase. When you have the ability to delay gratification, will help in ensuring that you manage your money in a better way. It is advisable to out of large purchases, instead of sacrificing important things or tying a purchase to a credit card. This will help in evaluating if you really need the purchase or more time to do a price comparison. Ensure that you develop a habit of saving up instead of having a tendency to use credit cards; this will help in avoiding any interest on the cost price.

✔   Always limit the purchases that you do use your credit card. In situations whereby you run out of cash, chances are that you will end up using your credit card even if you cannot even afford the purchase and paying the balance. Learn to resist from using your credit cards when making any purchases that you know you cannot afford and especially on this that you do not need.

✔   Develop a habit of saving regularly. Open a savings account and ensure that you deposit money regularly; you can do it daily, weekly, or monthly depending on your income. This will definitely help in developing a healthier financial habit. Another better way will be to set up a plan that the funds are automatically credited to your account. That will help reduce the responsibility of reminding yourself to do that all the time.

✔   If you need to be a good manager
when it comes to money, ensure that
you practice it all the time. Plan
when you intend to make a purchase
and always buy what you can afford.
When you make it a routine and a
daily habit, it will be easier to
manage money and the better for
your finances.

Money Market Mistakes

To be successful in your investment
in the money market, you need to ask
yourself several questions/statements:

1. Do you have an account for emergencies?
2. The account that you have will be an investment
3. That the funds you are setting aside will be useful soon.

When you decide to invest, you need to know that it is a risky venture and there are factors that you will need to consider first before any investment. For instance, when you decide to invest in a stock you need to know of factors like economic volatility. In the case of bonds, there are challenges like interest rates and inflationary risks. For a brave investor, leaning on a money market account will be a brave move. This is because they are known for safekeeping for the money. There are several mistakes when it comes to money market:

✔ The mistake that most investors make is thinking that money market accounts are the same as money market funds. They are financial instruments that have distinctive differences. Most people know of the money market fund as a mutual fund, the main characteristics are low returns and risks for every investment. They invest their funds in liquid assets for example cash. When invested in debt securities they have higher returns and ratings and mature in a shorter time. Most investors make the mistake and think that their money is safer in the money market, but that is not the same as with money market funds.

✔   Most people who are in investment believe that the money that they have in the money market is safe. The biggest mistake that they make is thinking that they are even safer from investments. Another belief is that, it better to have a lower interest rate with money in the bank than no interest at all. Most investors do not know the exposure they are in regarding inflation. This is the main reason that funds that are in the money market will not beat inflation. A good example is when the inflation rate is low than the interest that is claimed. Investors would know that, even though they believe the money market is safe, they are not safe from inflation.

✔   When in investment, you always need to know how to strike the right balance. Most of the time, the money market is influenced by inflation changes and rates. When you have such an investment, do not be tempted to input higher capital. They need a higher minimum balance as compared to the normal savings accounts. The normal account needs to be in operation for at least one year and have a higher amount of capital. When you have anything more than that, then it will be sitting their idle and it will lose value.

✔   Most investors like using money as their safety blanket. They believe that when they hold onto their money, it will be the best approach for any investment. This is not true especially when it is about savings whether in their money market or standard savings. It is not right to have your money exposed to uncertainty and any risk. This is one of the reasons why investors are afraid to invest and they would rather stay with their cash.

✔   To be a good investor, you need to know about asset diversification.
When you are dealing with cash that is no different at all; this is because most people believe that cash is not an asset. You need to know that from the basics of finance and accounting, cash is known as a current asset.
When you decide to hold on cash, ensure you do not hold more than
$200k. It is not a coincidence to find

any ordinary investor who has several bank accounts, in order to secure their cash. They have an approach to divide money or cash into three categories and that is a useful thing. The first one is to ensure that you have some money set aside for at least 3 years that is considered a shorter period. Around 4 to 10 years as the average timeframe and above 10 years as the longest timeframe. This is what will help the investors to know how long they can time their projects, how much is needed, and what will be saved in the end. This approach is important because it will also help in knowing about all the risks.

The best advice is to ensure that you invest in investments that are in the long-term and on lower risks. These will include investments like bonds, treasury bonds, life insurance, and

annuity. You will need to know of
the options that will help to avoid
losing money value, avoiding any
risks and the different ways about
cash diversification. You can make
use of the different trading and
investment tools that will help in
giving more returns instead of
money market accounts. You need to
look for investments that will help in
creating more returns in a shorter
time than the longer timeframe.

✔   Any investor needs to know that the
     reason for the money market is to hold
     money. When you have your money in
     just one place, you will not have any
     earnings or benefits; you need to move
     the money around. You will need to
     get more information on the different
     options and invest more. You should
     also know that money market accounts
     are not to be considered as long-term

investments. The main reason is that they are subject to high interest rates than what is charged on a normal savings account. Hence not the reason to consider it a long-term investment.

✔   You should not be enticed to look for accounts that offer interest rates as a promotion. The reason is the interests are bound to change after some time.

Budgeting Apps

As an investor, you need to know that, with the tough economic times you need to know the best way to invest in the financial market. And when you become successful and start making money, you need to look for apps that will in managing your money. Thanks to technology all, those apps are easily available and easy to download. They can be downloaded and installed on tablets and smartphones, hence you can use them anytime and anywhere you are due to portability. The apps help is keeping you on track regarding the way you spend and how you spend.

✔ **Mint:**

Mint can be downloaded as an app or used as a website; it is in the budgeting and investment category. It is compatible with iOS, Web, Windows 8, and Android. It is more of a budgeting app and it will still help in managing your money. It has a feature whereby you can categorize and customize all your expenses and transactions. It has the ability to synchronize all your transactions from investments, bank accounts, and credit cards. They have a reminder feature for all your pending bills and this helps to avoid any lateness in bill payment that should be very convenient for any investor. All you need to do is set up a free account and then include all your financial details. This will then give a breakdown anytime an activity happens and you will be able to get a report.

✔ Good Budget:

This app uses the envelope concept, when you sign up you are given 10 free envelopes when you are on standard subscription. When you have an upgrade to Plus, you will then be charged a monthly charge of $6, and then you will have unlimited envelopes. The concept works in a way that, when your envelope is empty, you are not able to shop or spend any money. The other alternative is that you can move money among envelopes; this is because the app has the flexibility to use a common budget. You can share the budget with other people, the app is compatible with iPhone and all android devices.

✔ **Dollar Bird:**

This app also helps in money management; it manages future expenses and will remind you when you have payment dues. To set up and activate is free and it has additional premium features. Your budget will be broken down in a calendar form and your pending expenses will be visible. You have the chance to have all your transactions in categories that are color-coded and they will keep on adding up as you have repeated transactions. When you check on your utility bill and paycheck, they will be displayed there. You will be able to see all your current balance. What you can spend and still be on a budget. The main setback is that it does not synchronize will your bank accounts. The problem is you will need to manually enter all the transactions. The app is available for iOS users, Android, and the web. You will have the privilege to know about your income, expenses, and cash flow.

✔ **Expensify:**

This is considered an app and tool that is used to report expenses, track all receipts, and all the expenses that you have. The main advantage is that it helps in quick data entry and saves a lot of time doing data entry. You will have the opportunity to make all the entries in one click. This app is available for Android and iOS users, you will do all the capturing automatically and using OCR; this is a smart scan. All your reports are available by taking one picture and they are all uploaded and completed within a click. When you submit your expense, they get reimbursed faster and approvals are done very fast. When you use the app, you will be able to track all your expenses, categorize all of them, know the cost of all. All the expenses are consolidated and synchronized.

Chapter 9: How to Become a Successful Swing Trader

There are different ways of becoming successful in swing trading. These can be implemented by the use of different swing trading strategies.

Strategies Used to Be a Successful Swing Trader

Strategies are a set of guidelines that assist their traders on how to run their swing trading. Strategies are there to guide you on your journey by minimizing losses and protecting your trading capital.

Below are some of the detailed strategies to be implemented in swing trading in order to be successful.

✔ **Breakout Strategies.**

This is a type of strategy used by most traders in the swing market. The trader selects the best trade by checking on the behavior of a stock monitoring its volatility and fluctuations of its price. Most of the market trades selected are the ones that break their own level of resistance and level of support.

✔ **Breakdown Strategy.**

This is another type of swing trading strategy used for monitoring the best market trade that does not break out its level of resistance and support. It normally focuses on trade securities with lower prices in the market.

✔ **Options Strategy.**

Combining options with your swing trading enables you to decide whether to sell or purchase an option at a certain price within a specified period of time.

When the time of expiry reaches, without exercising on the option, you lose the initial amount of money you paid for.

✔   **Stuck in a Box.**

This swing trading strategy is all about identifying all the various market range which are lower than the level of support. It leads to the setting of the stop-loss order which enables the maximization of the trading capital.

✔   **Catch the Wave.**

This type of swing trading strategy identifies any move that comes up in the market. It basically monitors any trend that takes place in the market. Mostly concerned with the market trade with the 50 moving average having a bullish rejection price.

✔ **Fading the Moves.**

This is a type of swing trading strategy that enables you to do your things against what is supposed to be in the market. All you need to do is to find a stronger force into the level of resistance that is higher than the previous one. Monitor the prices and select the stronger price in the market.

✔ **Aligning Trade with the Market Direction.**

The behavior in the market varies a lot. You need to observe the different market trends happening in the market and go with the trends. Most of the traders select the long-term market trends for the maximum amount of capital. You can decide to form your own policies of trading based on the current changes in the market. This will enable you to do much research and be keen on all kinds of news feeds related to the type of trading you handling.

✔ Have More Strength Than a Weakness.

This strategy enables you to be wise when selecting the type of trades. It assists you in selecting the trades with the long term in bullish markets and trades with short term in bearish markets. This enables you to have high potential for high profits and minimize losses in your swing trading.

✔ Get Advantage of the Long-Term Swing Trading Charts.

This strategy enables you to not only monitor the short-term trends happening in the market but also the long-term trends with a duration such as weekly and monthly trading charts.

✔ Be Alert with the Market Trends.

This strategy helps in handling the trends taking place in the market. It considers both long term trends and short-term trends. It alerts you in case of any market trends that take place.

✔ Have a Trading Plan When Beginning Trading.

A trading plan is a simple swing trading strategy that all swing traders need to select. Having a trading plan strategy when starting off swing trading is the best strategy for any trader. A trading plan enables you to note down all your trading objectives and goals of your trading. It provides you with guidelines and organizes you. You are able to come up with even a time routine for making your trades.

A trader is able to know the trading estimates thereby offering protection to your trading capital. A trading plan also outlines all the tips and tricks for swing trading. It is a simple strategy that most traders are advised to implement.

It assists in risks and loss management. Why shouldn't you select a simple strategy like this? Be awoke and implement the simple strategies in your swing trading in order to be successful.

✔ **Have a Positive Attitude.**

Your attitude determines your performance at all times. You need to have a strategy of possessing a positive attitude when you are trading. A positive attitude in swing trading contributes to good spirit, psyche, and even happiness while trading. You need to be excited and fell motivated. Do not begin your morning trading with a sad face. You will not even be able to spot any trend on the market. Be joyful and positive that your trading will work out.

A positive attitude will also enable you to be alert and keen on market trends. You will have the psyche to make trades and make good decisions even on your worst-case scenarios in the market. Put a smile on your face and wish yourself the best in swing trading by possessing a good attitude.

How to Use Moving Averages

Moving averages are basically trading tools that are commonly used by most swing traders in various trading activities in the market. Moving strategies cannot really be described as simple as they sound like. Moving strategies require much learning before implementing them because they are quite complicated and which need sufficient mastering for them to be fully utilized by a trader. Various mistakes are normally committed by most traders when they are trying to implement the various moving tools as one of their strategies in getting large amounts of profits in swing trading activities. There exist two major kinds of moving averages tools in the swing trading market; the exponential moving average and the simplified moving average. A trader is encouraged to select the kind of moving average he or she would like to engage with in advance before commencing any swing trading activities.

This is much expected because different tools normally bear different ways of operations that a particular should master and utilize in every kind of strategy that is likely to be involved. Let us venture into some of the factors which a potential trader should consider when choosing the preferred moving averages tools to implement in his or her swing trading activities:

✔ **The Difference Between the Exponential Moving Average and the Simplified Moving Average.**

There exists a common difference between the two moving averages which is the rate of speed in which they operate. The exponential moving average is quite faster as compared to the simplified moving average in swing trading and changes its direction much drastically as compared with the simplified moving average.

The exponential moving average highlights its immediate changes faster and much boldly rather than the simplified moving average which really takes some amount of time to highlight some of its recent market updates and the general changes that have been experienced in the swing trading market.

Quite a number of traders have engaged themselves in the exponential moving average because they claim to consider it much reliable and the trader is able to spot out the latest market feeds concerning the market. Updated market feeds depicted from the market inform

the trader of the actual status of activities
that are happening in the market and the
trader gets to remain informed and the
market volatility rates.

✔ The Advantages and Disadvantages of the Moving Averages.

The potential trader ought to pick the
kind of moving average that totally
seems to work out for a particular kind of
trader. This can be achieved if he or she
gets to highlight the various advantages
and disadvantages of each kind of
moving average in swing trading and
confirming the specific kind of moving
average that seems to work well for a
specific kind of swing trader. As
discussed, the exponential moving
average seems to be quite faster in
pronouncing the changes that have been
made in the swing trading market as
compared to the simplified moving
average. This justifies that the
exponential moving average is quite

191

vulnerable in giving out the wrong signs at a very early stage during trading. Wrong signals that have been pronounced at such occurrences may cause the inconsistent trader in making the wrong decisions just based on the current market trends and therefore causing large amounts of losses to be made that may eventually lead to a great financial breakdown.

On the other hand, the simplified market average which is much slower as compared to the exponential market average may take quite a while in the market when there exist market price movements that have been short-lived.

However, the simplified moving average gets a trader involved in swing trading much later as compared to the exponential moving average hence a trader is able to discover the changes later in the market, an event which may cause the trader to miss out on the good opportunities present in the market that might get grasped earlier by the other traders.

✔ **Weighing and Confirming the Right Kind of Moving Average.** Noting down the various advantages and disadvantages of the moving averages help a particular trader to decide on what he or she really wants. We have concluded that the simplified moving average spotlights the market trends at a later period, therefore outputting a lot of late results that may be so wrong when compared with the current actual market happenings, a case that is normally an effect caused by the volatility of the market.

On the other hand, the exponential moving average is usually depicted at a quite faster rate since the signs are normally expressed immediately and the trader gets to spot on the actual status of the market happenings. The signals are however said to be much vulnerable, an occurrence that can lead to wrong results due to the day market volatility that has been affecting the market. As a trader, try your best to pick out the best one that totally works for you, that is, much efficient and one that can easily be implemented to acquire larger amounts of profits.

✔   **Choosing the Best Period Setting.**

After selecting the favorable kind of moving average that a particular trader finds it more efficient, he or she now ought to find out the best period setting that he or she finds much satisfying to offer the best signals. First things first, the trader in question is expected to know the main reason behind the use of the various movement agencies in his or her swing trading activities.

Most experienced traders prefer using the kind of period settings moving averages that are much common and famous to most traders. The novice traders are recommended to go with the market flow when choosing the best period setting which really works for them.

Below are some of the periods that most swing traders get involved in:

- **The 20 or 21 trading period.**

This particular trading period is mostly recommended to the short-term kind of traders with particular shorter time frames. This trading period is termed to outline easily the various trade shifts that are happening in the swing trading market.

- **The 50 periods.**

The 50 periods are believed to be so much popular in the swing trading market and very much standard since it is the definite compromise between the much long and much short kind of trades.

- **The 100 periods.**

This one is used by traders who normally engage in the daily and weekly time frames. It is believed to offer so much support and good resistance to the trader during swing trading.

- **The 200 or 250 periods.**

This type of period is also famous in swing trading. It basically describes the price action in an entire trading year.

Chapter 10: Common Mistakes to Avoid in Swing Trading

Mistakes are always part of the game in any trading. Traders in swing trading make mistakes too that make them not succeed. Others commit the mistakes due to ignorance of the different rules and strategies used in swing trading.

This section is all about giving details of the various mistakes committed by the different traders in swing trading.

Mistakes That Swing Traders Make

Below are the various mistakes swing traders commit while trading:

✔ **Lacking a Trading Plan.**

Most of the traders starting off on swing trading lack a well-defined plan. What do you normally think of when you do this? Swing trading is a risky arena. You need to be well-armed and prepared before entering into trading. Lacking a proper trading plan makes you misbehave in your trading which is a very bad idea.

You normally lack a trading routine when you fail to have a plan. You find yourself lacking the objectives and goals for your trading. A trading plan enables you to stick to the plan and work hard for your objectives. Failing to have a plan makes you do things when you feel like it is so risky in the swing trading environment.

A plan is basically composed of objectives and strategies. Without it, it is like going for a war with no weapons with you. Prepare yourself with a good plan to be able to know the risks involved in the market since it enables you to formulate your own trading strategies.

✔   **Lacking a Time Horizon for Your Trading.**

Always know as a swing trader the duration you have for investment reasons. It enables you to be aware of the time duration you have before expiry. When you select your time horizon to be until retirement, it tells that you have to invest for a while before the time of retirement.

✔   **Failing to Utilize the Stop-Loss Orders.**

Stop-loss orders are very crucial for all kinds of traders. You need to implement it for safety reasons during trading. A trader who fails to utilize stop-loss orders strategies ends up with huge losses on their trading. You find yourself making big losses that could be controlled. Losses all times turn down the success of any business. Failing to arm yourself so well in trading is just a total failure for your swing trading. You need to be alert with the crucial strategies in swing trading so as to survive and succeed.

✔ Lacking Control over the Trading Losses.

Losses will normally occur in most businesses, but does that mean you should have no control over them? You need to make fast and efficient actions when losses occur in your swing trading, even the smaller losses. Ignoring the smaller losses will make them accumulate so hard and time will reach you will have no control over them. You need to be serious about the losses that come up and be able to handle them before they shut down your trading. Losses promote no growth in swing trading. You need to have policies with you on how to handle losses. Most of the traders neglect this mistake which makes them fail in swing trading tremendously.

✔ **Putting Much Trust in Financial News.**

Watching and following up on news is not a bad thing, however, you need to be extra careful with what you hear or come across online. Some bloggers mislead the novice traders a lot on how to handle their trading. You should be alert with all the information. Some people just want to see fail. Do not apply all the information you hear from other people. Have your own ways of how to handle things in swing trading. You do not need to copy what others are doing, people have different abilities. Rely only on the trusted sources and swing trading forums. Consult the experts in swing trading for any information that you have heard and you are not sure about it. Have trust in yourself that your ways will also succeed in swing trading.

✔ **Working on Too Many Markets at Once.**

A high number of swing traders fail in

their trading due to being over- occupied with too many markets at once. You are not like a robot machine, you need to decide on a reasonable amount of markets that you can handle. Do not be greedy for money, you need to calm down and at least focus on a few and perfect your skills rather than being involved with too many markets. This will make you get out of control. Concentrating on many markets is even not healthy for your body and mind. You do need to select every market. You should choose the ones you are highly interested in, perfect your skills on them and ace swing trading.

✔ Being Overconfident.

Being a confident swing trader is a good thing, but being extra than that is really a poor thing to do. Overconfidence has killed the dream of many swing traders. Traders are normally over certain with what they are doing and fail to list down even the risks that may be involved in their trading. You need to remember both the worst-case and the best-case scenarios in swing trading while planning. Consult others when you need help with your strategies, you may learn a few things that will help you in your trading. Do not be that kind of a bold trader who does things alone with no trainer or some sort of master in swing trading. Do not trust yourself that much, you might be doing things the wrong way.

✔ **Lack of Patience.**

Good things take time. This saying is also relevant in our case here. Most traders have no patience at all of the huge profits. They only want money to be accumulated in the first days after joining swing trading. That is not possible unless all you want to accumulate are huge losses. You need to give yourself more time before you begin to earn more money.

The kind of traders who rush in trading for their greedy for money end up nowhere. You need to be realistic sometimes to succeed in swing trading. Do not be on the rush in trading, the money will still come. Do the right thing at the right speed. Do not implement many strategies on your trading and get confused. Work at least with one successful trading strategy and be relaxed.

✔ **Indiscipline.**

Being indiscipline in swing trading is not advised. Success is directly related to discipline. When you are disciplined in your trading, you are able to handle your trade with cautious and with the right mindset. Traders who mix their trading procedures and activities with other things end up mixing everything up. You need to be aware of all of your strategies and objectives at your fingertips to be able to know what you want to achieve. Not being disciplined makes you even forget your targets and your policies. This, of course, leads to total failure in your trading.

✔ Too Much Focus on Profit.

Profit-making is one of the main objectives of all businesses, but why focus too much on profit and forget about other crucial factors in swing trading? Factors like risk management and loss handling losses also need attention. Do not be the kind of traders who just think of making a profit and end up making big losses in their trading.

You need to have a balance on how you handle your trading activities. Do not allow to accumulate high profits which have the same amount as losses.

There will no earn since the losses
made will decline both your trading
capital and your profits.

✔ Failing to Trust Your Abilities.

You need to have trust in your
capabilities. As a beginner, you should
not compare yourself with the expert
successful traders. This will make your
esteem to decline. You need to be
yourself and remind yourself that you
will succeed. All you need to do is to
comply with the strategies and objectives
that you wrote down. You also need to
learn a lot and do much research in swing
trading in order to succeed.

✔ Using Much Money on the Investment.

The amount of money you are
dedicating for investment should be a
good amount of your disposable income
that you can quickly or easily refund.
Utilize a little money at the beginning to

avoid huge losses. The higher the amount of money you use for swing trading, the higher the number of losses that can come up due to the many risks that are involved in swing trading.

Most traders boast around with a huge amount of cash for trading and unfortunately end up making huge losses. Also, do not trade with your school fees or rent, you will have issues with your school finance.

✔ Being Emotional on the Money Lost.

Catching feelings in trading are not advised for any swing traders. Some traders give up when losses occur and decide to quit. Do not be faint-hearted trader you need to be strong that the money lost will get refunded. Stand strong and wish yourself good luck.

✔ Being Too Much Aggressive.

Most unsuccessful swing traders failed to

succeed because of their aggressive behavior. Being aggressive makes you lose a lot of money which leads to the failure of swing trading. This normally happens on a bullish type of market. Relax and everything will work out.

✔ **Laziness and Being Irresponsible.**

All types of trading are tough. You need to put much effort into your swing trading in order to widen your knowledge. Failing to do much research will not keep you informed and updated. You need to go with the trend. Do not be left behind. Failing to go through different newsfeeds on swing trading will enable you to be outdated.

Irresponsible swing traders who lack trading plans and strategies get confused and finally decide to quit swing trading. You need to be responsible and make decisions even during the worst-case scenarios. Do not fail to work even on the small losses that occur during swing trading. Trade responsibly bearing in mind all of the risks involved in swing trading.

✔ Ignoring Risk Management Trading Strategies.

What do you expect when you fail to implement the few strategies needed for risk management? Swing traders who fail to implement the risk management strategies of course end up being involved with too many risks. You need to check on the different swing trading strategies that exist and choose the best that handles risks in swing trading. This will protect your trading capital and also the amount of profit accumulated. Failing to arm yourself well enough will bring failure to your trading.

✔ Implementing Many Small Moves.

This mistake is normally committed by

the novice traders who make moves on
any small changes in the market. You
find yourself making trades even on your
weakest points. There are high chances of
big losses during this time.

You need to be extra cautious and only
make sure moves when relevant changes
occur in the market. Small moves
contribute to huge losses. Trade at the
right time according to your trading plan.
Avoid this mistake in order to succeed in
swing trading.

✔   **Being so Close to the Market.**

Traders who focus so much on the swing
trading market end up living in worries all
the time. You end up putting much effort
even on small things that need less
attention. Do something else other than
trading. You can even do some cooking or
even water flowers. Give yourself some
time to catch a breath with a good mindset
that everything will work out well. Do not

be so close to the market, you will worry
too much for nothing.

✔ **Lacking a Swing Trading Strategy.**

Strategies are like guidelines that exist in swing trading to help you when making decisions.
Most of the swing traders forget to
formulate the trading strategies when
formulating the swing trading plan.
Lacking swing trading strategies is a very
bad idea. Strategies help you in managing
risks and accumulating more profit. Always
stick to your working strategies that are
according to your trading plan.

Chapter 11: Terminologies Used in Swing Trading

This final chapter is all about going through the different terms used in swing trading markets.

Swing Trading Glossary

The swing trading glossary consists of the following terms:

✔ **ADX.**

This is an abbreviation for the Average Directional Index in swing trading. It is an indicator used in technical analysis to determine how powerful a trend is. The indicator can either be positive or negative. It also helps a trader to decide whether to take a long or short trade. Average Directional Index was developed by Welles Wilder and shows that a trend is powerful when it has an

ADX above 25. Contrarily, the trend is less powerful when it has an ADX below 20.

✔ **A Priori.**

This normally means the act of using information or data from the previous time in trading to make predictions on the current behavior of trades in the current time.

✔ **Alert.**

Alert is a feature used in most of the swing trading platforms and software to inform the trader in case of any changes in the market. It alerts the trader by sending either an email or a text message when an event has occurred.

✔ **Algorithm.**

An algorithm is a computer program designed to execute trades based on the inputs provided. The inputs can be even technical indicators and newsfeeds. They make trading be efficient and of good quality.

✔ **Ask.**

This is the price normally used by swing sellers to demand in the market. This price is normally higher than the price the buyer wants to buy. It promotes profit-making in your swing trading.

✔ **Backtesting.**

This is the process of testing on a swing trading strategy you have come up with in order to be sure that the strategy is going to work out. Once the strategy works out well, a trader implements it on trading for huge profits.

✔ **Bar Chart.**

Bar chart is a simple charting technique that displays the different price range of swing trading with a certain time range. Bar charts are available in most of the online trading platforms.

✔ **Bear Market.**

This is a market situation where the prices of either the stock and commodities are expected to decline within a specified period of time. They sustain for several months or even years. Bear markets can either be cyclical or secular. The cyclical ones last for several months of the year while the secular ones last for several decades.

✔   Bid.

This is the kind of price that buyers quote when they want to purchase a certain stock at a certain price in the market. The bid price is normally lower than the market price of the market. This price normally rises when there are some negotiations between the seller and the buyer in the market.

✔   Breakout.

This is the point where the price of the stock in the market moves out of the desired estimates. It is normally past the level of resistance and below the level of support.

✔   Broker.

An authorized individual or company that offers trading services to traders of a market. The trading services may include trading platforms that traders use to post their market trades depending on the trends. A broker also assists the traders with any issues arising from the trading platforms in terms of system failure. They charge commissions to the traders who utilize their services for trading in the market.

✔ Bull Market.

This is a market situation where the prices of market trades are expected to rise. The market trades that are expected to rise in price are mostly bonds and stocks. Bull markets sustain for months and even years.
It takes place mostly when the economy in the country is strong in terms of low unemployment rates and even high income among individuals.

✔   **Buying Long.**

Buying long in the market refers to purchasing a commodity with the expectation that it will rise in price. Normally happens to traders who do not expect to offer the asset for sale after a short while.

✔   **Capital Losses.**

This refers to the losses that come up when you offer a capital asset for sale at a price lower than its price at the beginning. This normally happens when the capital asset reduces its value. The capital assets may be investment or even real estate.

✔ **Cover.**

This is a kind of insurance strategy in swing trading. You purchase a cover when you want to protect your stock from the volatility in the market. This protects the stock from any kind of risk in the market.

✔   **Downtrend.**

This refers to the action where the price of market security declines in its price within a specified period of time. The action is normally described by the low peaks and low troughs in a charting platform.

✔   **Entry Point.**

This is the point in the market where you become aware of the pattern changes in the market. It helps in risk management in the market and protects your trading capital.

✔ **Exit Point.**

This point is normally the escape strategy implemented when you want to get rid of the position in your market security. It can either be the point that targets profits in your trading or else the stop-loss point which assists to minimize all kinds of losses in your trading.

✔ Float.

Float is the number of shares of a company or any business that is available for trading.

✔ Forex.

This is a type of market in trading that involves the trade of foreign exchange. It is one of the largest markets in swing trading.

✔ Indicator.

This is a numeric value that comes from a mathematic computation. It normally arises due to any price changes or any changes affected by stock. Most of the traders are advised to set their own indicators that assist in trade execution. They help in predicting the performance of your trading.

✔   **Investing.**

Investing is the process of buying a particular asset with the expectation that it will increase in its value after a certain period of time. The period of time can either be long term or short term.

✔   **Limit Order.**

A type of order in swing trading where you are able to sell or purchase an asset in the market at a lower price than the price in the market. It guarantees you that you will pay for the asset at a lower price. Limit orders are normally integrated with a stop-loss order to prevent huge losses during trading.

✔   **Liquidity.**

This term indicates the amount of volume available in stock. You are able to know the amount of profit you will accumulate when you are either beginning or closing your trading. Most of the swing trading investors utilize this factor of liquidity when making their own decisions for better performance in the swing market.

✔ Market Order.

This is a type of imposing request as an investor to a broker to offer you an asset for sale at a better price available in the swing market. Most traders use market orders since you can easily get in and out of the market. It has a lower commission since less task is done in the market when you implement market orders on your trading. Market orders are applied in market securities with higher volumes.

✔ Market Volatility.

Market volatility is mostly concerned with observing the various changes that occur in the price of the assets. Volatility is measured by the use of different pricing models and also the beta coefficients. It predicts the behavior of the stock's price. The more volatile market security is, the riskier it becomes as compared to the less volatile assets.

✔ **Margin.**

This is the amount of money a broker lends you for trading preferably for purchasing different market securities. The market securities act as the collateral for the loan given by the brokers.

✔ **Mid-day.**

This is a time duration in swing trading around 1100 hours to 1400 hours EST. At this time, the price of the market securities normally drops at this time but finally rises later on in the market.

✔ **Paper Trading.**

This is a method used in swing trading

where beginners try out the mock accounts which provide virtual accounts with virtual money for trading practice. The accounts assist in working on your skills and perfecting them before getting into the real world of swing trading. The paper trading helps traders in finding the favorite trades and also the swing brokers.

✔ **Profit Target.**

A profit target is a point of acting as an exit point when your trading opportunities bring up profits in your trading. This point is normally generated when you study your trading charts and be able to identify the best type of trade by calculating their rewards and risks.

✔ **Risk Management.**

This is all about the methods associated with managing all the risks in your swing trading. The methods may include the implementation of the stop-loss orders and also the limit orders. Risk management promotes the generation of huge profits for your trading and also protects your trading capital.

✔ Short Selling.

Happens mostly when you borrow shares from your swing broker and offer them for sale with high expectations that the price of the market security will drop and it will be bought at the lower price. Profit is kept when you take the shares back to your broker.

✔ Stop-Loss Order.

This is the type of order which acts as an indicator by showing the level you are supposed to be to prevent incurring bigger losses in your swing trading. You need to have this strategy to protect your trading capital and be able to minimize your trading losses.

✔   **Swing Trading.**

This is a type of trading that offers assets such as stock for sale that you hold for a long time like weeks. It is a unique type of trading as compared to options and day trading.

✔   **Trading Plan.**

This is a set of guidelines that help you in how you coordinate your swing trading. It entails the goals, objectives and even your own strategies. It assists in disciplining you and you even able to generate a routine of how to do your trading. A trading plan is normally formulated when you are starting off with your swing trading. It also consists of an escape plan and the entry point which help in loss management. You need to always have a trading plan with you in order to succeed in swing trading.

✔ **Trading Software.**

This is an online swing trading platform provided by your swing broker. It enables you to make your trades and even make predictions on your trades. It has different features to help you in your swing trading. Features such as the

charting platforms help you read the bar charts and observe the price change behavior. Newsfeeds and research tools are also available on most of the trading software.

Traders are normally advised to select the trading software with a friendly user interface.

The ones you can control and handle on your own with no trouble. Swing trading software has varying prices as it depends on the quality of the platform and also your broker.

✔   **Uptrend.**

This refers to the action where the price
of market security rises in its price
within a specified period of time. The
action is normally described by the high
peaks and high troughs in a charting
platform.

✔   **Volume.**

This is the overall amount of all the
contracts or shares of certain security that
is offered for trade within a specified
period of time.

Conclusion

At this point you can comfortably start swing trading, you know of the capital needed, how much income an individual can make, the daily routine of a swing trader and the whole process of starting swing trading. There are tips that you should ensure that you use when you start trading and apply all the tools and techniques that you have learned. Money management is a concept that needs a lot of commitment and focus, apply the basic, the importance, the skills that you will need to adapt, the world top money managers, the mistakes that you will need to avoid and the useful apps that will help in budgeting and money management.

9 781803 615776